Fodor's InFocus

ARUBA

W9-AYF-091

Fodor's InFocus ARUBA

Publisher: Stephen Horowitz, *General Manager*

Editorial: Douglas Stallings, *Editorial Director*; Jill Fergus, Amanda Sadlowski, Caroline Trefler, *Senior Editors*; Kayla Becker, Alexis Kelly, *Editors*; Angelique Kennedy-Chavannes, *Assistant Editor*

Design: Tina Malaney, *Director of Design and Production*; Jessica Gonzalez, *Graphic Designer*

Production: Jennifer DePrima, *Editorial Production Manager*; Elyse Rozelle, *Senior Production Editor*; Monica White, *Production Editor*

Maps: Rebecca Baer, *Senior Map Editor*; David Lindroth, Ed Jacobus, William Wu, with additional cartography provided by Henry Columb, Mark Stroud, and Ali Baird, Moon Street Cartography, *Cartographers*

Photography: Viviane Teles, *Senior Photo Editor*; Namrata Aggarwal, Payal Gupta, Ashok Kumar, *Photo Editors*; Rebecca Rimmer, *Photo Production Associate*; Eddie Aldrete, *Photo Production Intern*

Business and Operations: Chuck Hoover, *Chief Marketing Officer*; Robert Ames, *Group General Manager*; Devin Duckworth, *Director of Print Publishing*

Public Relations and Marketing: Joe Ewaskiw, *Senior Director of Communications and Public Relations*

Fodors.com: Jeremy Tarr, *Editorial Director*; Rachael Levitt, *Managing Editor*

Technology: Jon Atkinson, *Director of Technology*; Rudresh Teotia, *Lead Developer*; Jacob Ashpis, *Content Operations Manager*

Writer: Susan Campbell

Editor: Alexis Kelly

Production Editor: Jennifer DePrima

8th Edition

ISBN 978-1-64097-471-5

ISSN 1939-988X

SPECIAL SALES

This book is available at special discounts for bulk purchases for sales promotions or premiums. For more information, e-mail SpecialMarkets@fodors.com.

PRINTED IN CANADA

10 9 8 7 6 5 4 3 2 1

About Our Writer

 Sue Campbell is an award-winning travel-and-lifestyle writer specializing in the Dutch Caribbean. She has hundreds of articles to her credit about Aruba, Bonaire, Curaçao, and St. Maarten in over 22 major national and international print and Web outlets as well as on-island magazines. When Susan isn't seeking the best hot spots in the tropics, she is reporting about the highlights of her hometown in Montreal. She updated the entire Aruba guide, as well as the Aruba, Bonaire, Curaçao, and Saba content of *Fodor's Essential Caribbean 2nd.*

Welcome to Aruba

The pastel houses of Dutch settlers still grace the waterfront in Oranjestad, Aruba's (known as "One Happy Island") capital city. Palm Beach, the island's main tourist hub, is home to beachfront high-rise hotels, dining, shopping, and entertainment. The low-rise hotels, and broadest stretches of white sand, are found along Eagle, Manchebo, and Druif Beaches. Winds are fierce, even savage, on the north coast, where you'll find cacti, rocky desert, and wind-bent divi-divi trees. On the west coast, steady breezes attract windsurfers to the shallow, richly colored waters.

TOP REASONS TO GO

★ **Beaches:** Powdery beaches and turquoise waters or wild waves crashing rocky cliffs.

★ **Nightlife:** Dance-till-you-drop spots and party buses like the Kukoo Kunuku make this island move after dark.

★ **Restaurants:** International fare and local snack hideaways offer foodies much to discover.

★ **Casinos:** Aruba's modern casinos will please both casual and serious gamblers.

★ **The Welcome:** A friendly multilingual population guarantees smiles everywhere you go.

Contents

Chapter 1

EXPERIENCE
ARUBA

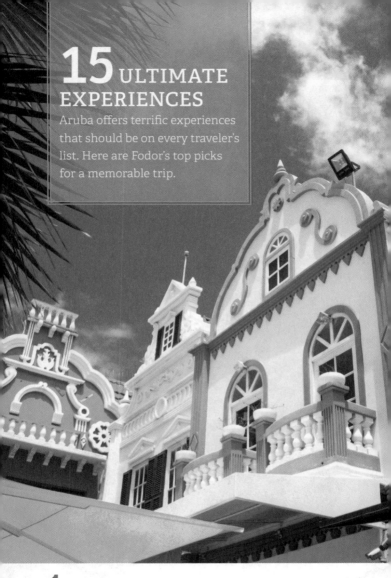

15 ULTIMATE EXPERIENCES

Aruba offers terrific experiences that should be on every traveler's list. Here are Fodor's top picks for a memorable trip.

1 Awesome Oranjestad

The colorful capital is easily explored on the free Downtown Trolley. Take a downtown walking tour or see free live entertainment at Renaissance Marketplace. (Ch. 3)

2 Stunning Eagle Beach

This stunning expanse of powder-soft sand and cerulean sea often tops best beach lists for its sheer beauty and pristine condition. And, it's home to Aruba's iconic tree, so get your selfie sticks ready. (Ch. 4)

3 Action-packed Casinos

If you like to gamble, or want to try your hand at a game or two, Aruba's casinos are the real deal, with options ranging from big, glitzy, Las Vegas–style affairs to intimate little gaming rooms. (Ch. 3, 4, 5)

4 San Nicolas Art Walk

Everywhere you look on San Nicolas's main streets, buildings are covered with beautiful murals. The art walk is free to explore on your own, but guided tours are available through Aruba Mural Tours. (Ch. 6)

5 Palm Beach Pleasures

One of the world's most popular beaches, Palm Beach is where you'll find many of the Caribbean's most cosmopolitan resorts, deluxe spas, fine restaurants, glittery casinos, and superb swimming. (Ch.5)

6 Explore Arikok National Park

Aruba's wild side isn't all parties. Stop by the visitor center and join one of the free guided hikes with a park ranger, or book a jeep tour with DePalm Tours. (Ch. 7)

7 Retail Therapy

There are ample opportunities to purchase fine jewelry, quality timepieces, high-end brand-name fashions, and Cuban cigars throughout Oranjestad and Palm Beach. (Ch. 3, 5)

8 Paseo Herencia

Located on the Palm Beach tourist strip, Paseo Herencia has restaurants, artisan kiosks, and a nightly magical light and water show in its fountain that's worth a visit. (Ch. 5)

9 Outstanding Scuba Diving

Advanced and novice divers appreciate the plentiful marine life and abundance of wrecks in Aruba's clear waters. There are even guided night dives, deep dives, and shore dives. (Ch. 8)

10 Above-Water Adventures

There are plenty of ways to spend time upon Aruba's aqua waves—party day sails, sunset voyages, dinner cruises, sailing, stand-up paddleboarding, sea kayaking, deep-sea fishing, and Splash Park. (Ch. 8)

11 World-Class Dining

For such a tiny island, Aruba has a large and eclectic food scene: romantic toes-in-the-sand spots, intimate chef's tables, culinary walking tours, or food and wine festivals. (Ch. 3, 4, 5, 6)

12 A Flurry of Festivals

Whether you like food, music, dancing, or art, Aruba has a festival for it. The island's longest-standing event is the weekly Bonbini Festival, but Carnival is the island's biggest celebration.(Ch. 2)

13 Barhopping Buses

Aruba's crazy barhopping buses offer a wild ride replete with stops at popular nightclubs and bars to give visitors a real feel for island nightlife. The bright red Kukoo Kunuku buses are an iconic sight. (Ch. 2)

14 Horseback Riding on Special Steeds

Aruba's rough-and-tumble interior is often best explored on horseback. Some tours lead to interesting landmarks like the ruins of a gold mine, and there are tours for all skill levels and ages. (Ch. 8)

15 Superb Snorkeling

With water visibility down to 90 feet, and warm waters full of marine life and colorful coral, snorkelers can often view the same wonders as divers, without the PADI certification. (Ch. 8)

WHAT'S WHERE

1 Oranjestad. Aruba's capital is a great place to go for shopping, restaurants, and nightlife.

2 Eagle, Druif, and Manchebo beaches. The island's "low-rise" hotel area offers miles of beautiful beach that's not overdeveloped but is dominated by the sprawling Divi complex.

3 Palm Beach, Noord, and Western Tip. The island's high-rise hotels and condos are found in Palm Beach in the district of Noord. The quiet and remote Western Tip is anchored by the California Lighthouse.

4 Arikok National Park and Environs. Nearly 20% of Aruba is covered by this sprawling national park. The small town of Santa Cruz, in the interior, gives a sense of how real Arubans live.

5 Savaneta and San Nicolas. The tiny fishing village of Savaneta was the first Dutch beachhead on Aruba and now holds some exclusive stays and dining surprises, while San Nicolas, once headquarters of the island's oil industry, has been totally reborn with public art.

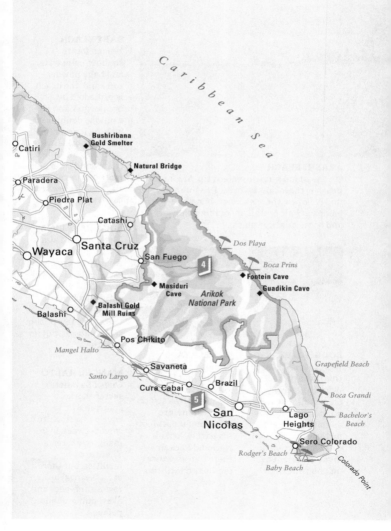

Aruba's Best Beaches

ARASHI BEACH
On the island's northwestern tip, Arashi Beach is the locals' favorite. Pristine and undeveloped, there's a beach bar, some palapas, chair rentals, an outdoor shower, and occasional live music.

BABY BEACH
Named for its shallow, calm waters and baby powder–soft sand, the beach is protected by a breakwater and has a unique double reef, making it great for kids or snorkeling; snorkel gear, lounge chairs, and sunshade tents can be rented. You can also see sea turtles.

BOCA CATALINA
Just north of Palm Beach, this little cove is easily accessible by car or public bus. The crystalline water makes it a favorite with snorkelers; there are a few public shade palapas, but no facilities.

RODGER'S BEACH
Next to Baby Beach, this is the perfect place to get away from it all. The water is shallow and clear as glass; there are no facilities, but you can rent snorkel or dive equipment at neighboring Baby Beach.

DOS PLAYA
It's not a swimmable spot, but Dos Playa's two beaches, separated by a swath of limestone, are ideal for sunbathing. It's part of Arikok National Park so there's an entrance fee, but no facilities.

MANGEL HALTO
One of Savaneta's secret snorkel spots, this little cove has soft white sand between lush mangrove forests. There are no facilities, but there are a few nearby restaurant–bars and a few public shade palapas.

Mangel Halto

EAGLE BEACH
Consistently listed as one of the world's best beaches, the stunning alabaster soft white sand meets an ever-changing wave of cerulean-hued ocean. There are a few stretches with motorized water sports, but it's best for romanticwalks and sunset viewing.

PALM BEACH
Studded with high-rise hotels, entertainment venues, and tourist attractions of every ilk, this is Aruba's best-known beach. Its shallow, clear, pond-calm surf and soft white sand also make it one of the island's best for water sports and young children.

DRUIF BEACH
This lovely half-mile stretch of sand is the main beach for the Divi Aruba All-Inclusive property. Wave action is medium, making it good for children, though the surf is restless at times. There's a public beach bar and plenty of food and drink options in the Alhambra Mall.

SURFSIDE BEACH
This little stretch of sand could almost be called an urban beach, as it's very near downtown Oranjestad. There are chair and umbrella rentals, the small Surf Side Beach Bar with changing facilities, and lovely sunset views.

BOCA GRANDI
Just outside of San Nicolas, this is the island's best kiteboarding spot. It's not really a swimmers' beach, as the current and waves are strong, and there are no facilities or shade palapas; bring your own food and drink and a beach blanket.

Aruba's Top Resorts

BUCUTI & TARA BEACH RESORT

This legendary adults-only property on Eagle Beach often tops "most romantic stays in the Caribbean" lists. The Tara Penthouse Suites are the epitome of luxe with deep soaking tubs, spacious balconies, and full kitchens.

THE RITZ-CARLTON ARUBA

The Ritz-Carlton name is synonymous with luxury on every level, but if you're really looking to splurge, the penthouse Ritz-Carlton Suite comes with a dedicated concierge and personal beach and pool service.

ARUBA OCEAN VILLAS

Secreted away in the tiny village of Savaneta, be prepared for absolute enchantment at this boutique luxury property, a collection of overwater bungalows, stunning beach villas, and even a two-story tree house.

DIVI ARUBA BEACH RESORT AND TAMARIJN ARUBA BEACH RESORT

These side-by-side all-inclusives, on the lovely and kid-friendly Druif and Divi Beaches, share access to dining, bars, entertainment, and water sports.

HOTEL RIU PALACE ARUBA

This family-friendly all-inclusive sits on Palm Beach. Kids love the royal Middle Eastern castle design, but the sprawling multi-level water circuit and comprehensive buffet (including a sundae bar and a chocolate fountain) are also big draws.

HILTON ARUBA CARIBBEAN

The Hilton's spacious beachfront is well designed with all kinds of pools and water circuits that lead to lush tropical nooks.

Hilton Aruba Caribbean Resort & Casino

HYATT REGENCY ARUBA RESORT, SPA AND CASINO

Magnificent faux ruins with a cascading waterfall that empties into a koi pond inhabited by black swans—this scene has always given the Hyatt a classy edge, and the new adults-only pool adds to its allure.

RENAISSANCE OCEAN SUITES

Located in downtown Oranjestad, this family-friendly property has large suites with kitchens, two pools, and a man-made beach with a breakwater to keep the surf swimmer-friendly. Plus, there's access to Renaissance Private Island and its famous flamingos.

HOLIDAY INN BEACH RESORT

Located on a stellar stretch of Palm Beach, the super-calm surf and soft sand in front of the sprawling hotel attracts families in droves, yet never seems crowded. The junior suites are perfect for families since they have small kitchenettes.

DIVI ARUBA PHOENIX BEACH RESORT

Self-caterers love this resort for its communal barbecues and spacious one-, two-, or three-bedroom suites that have an in-room washer/dryer and full kitchens. There's a children's pool with daily activities, and gentle surf ideal for little ones.

Aruba's Best Outdoor Activities

GREAT GOLFING
Whether you're learning the game or already love it, Aruba has some great courses including the Robert Trent Jones Jr.–designed Tierra del Sol, the island's premiere 18-hole golf course.

EXPLORE OUTDOOR ART
San Nicolas is filled with outdoor art installations, murals, and more. Walk the grid on your own or take a tour with Aruba Mural Tours.

EXPLORE BY BIKE
The paved Linear Park—from downtown Oranjestad to the airport—has made biking very popular. Explore it on rentable electric bikes or through the island's bike share program; some resorts provide free coaster bikes.

SNORKEL OR SEA KAYAK
With calm, clear aqua waters teeming with tropical fish, there's plenty to see under the waves, including numerous shipwrecks. Sea kayaking is extra special when you go in glass-bottomed boats around the mangroves in Mangel Halto.

WINDSURFING AND KITEBOARDING
With shallow waters and constant gentle winds, the conditions at Fishmen's Huts Beach are ideal for beginner windsurfers. Boca Grandi is a favorite hangout for kiteboarders, and the annual Aruba Hi-Winds event attracts international talent.

DEEP-SEA FISHING
Chartered boats are available for half- or full-day excursions to catch anything from barracuda and tuna to kingfish.

Windsurfing and kiteboarding

SCUBA DIVING

Aruba is known among divers as the Caribbean's wreck capital, and there are plenty of dive sites right offshore, some in very shallow water, that have helped the island earn its reputation. The island also has plenty of dive operators for novice and expert divers.

OFF-ROADING EXPLORATIONS

Aruba's interior is rugged and rocky and best explored with an ATV, especially if you want to explore the cacti-studded countryside or visit incredible landmarks like the small natural bridges, the natural pool, or the wild coast. Tours can be booked with De Palm Tours and ABC Tours.

ARIKOK PARK HIKING

Explore the island's arid outback with a guided tour to unearth all the secrets of the park. Start at the park's visitor center; there's a small museum, café, and maps, and it's where the free, but short, park ranger-guided tours of the immediate area leave from.

HORSEBACK RIDING

Aruba has an interesting equine history that starts with Spanish explorers. There are trails and rides for all ages through interesting terrain like goldmine ruins and cacti-studded outback as well as along sand dunes and beautiful beaches.

Aruba Today

Arubans are proud of their autonomous standing within the Kingdom of the Netherlands, and Gilberto François "Betico" Croes is heralded as the hero behind the island's *status aparte* (separate status). His birthday, January 25, is an official Aruban holiday.

During the Dutch colonial expansion of the 17th century, Aruba and five other islands—Bonaire, Curaçao, St. Maarten, St. Eustatius, and Saba—became territories known as the Netherlands Antilles. After World War II these islands began to pressure Holland for autonomy, and in 1954 they became a collective self-governing entity under the umbrella of the Kingdom of the Netherlands.

At that time, several political parties were in power on the island. Soon, however, Juancho Irausquin (who has a major thoroughfare named in his honor) formed a new party that maintained control for nearly two decades. Irausquin was considered the founder of Aruba's new economic order and the precursor of modern Aruban politics. After his death his party's power diminished.

In 1971 Croes, then a young, ambitious school administrator, became the leader of another political party. Bolstered by a thriving economy generated by Aruba's oil refinery, Croes spearheaded the island's cause to secede from the Netherlands Antilles and to gain status as an equal partner within the Dutch kingdom. Sadly, he didn't live to celebrate the realization of his dream. On December 31, 1985, the day before Aruba's new status became official, Croes was in a car accident that put him in a coma for 11 months. He died on November 26, 1986. Etched in the minds of Arubans are his prophetic words: *Si mi cai na cominda, gara e bandera y sigui cu e lucha* ("If I die along the way, seize the flag and go on with the struggle").

On March 18, 1948, the Aruban politician Shon A. Eman put forth the first formal proposal for Aruba's independence from the Netherlands Antilles. Twenty-eight years later to the day, Croes declared the first National Anthem and Flag Day, a national holiday that celebrates Aruba's independence with parades, sporting and cultural events, and lots of food. Most shops, gas stations, and supermarkets are closed or close early.

Aruba has its own democratic constitution and its capital is in Oranjestad. The parliament consists of 21 elected members; the majority parties form a seven-member Council of Ministers that's headed by a prime minister for a four-year term. The reigning monarch of the Netherlands appoints a governor who holds office for a six-year term, and acts as her representative. In 2017, Aruba made history in appointing its first female prime minister, Evelyn Wever-Croes.

Today, the country is fairly stable, and the struggle is more about preserving the island's environmental legacy. Welcoming over 2 million visitors a year has taken a toll on the island's fragile ecosystem, and the government has been aggressive in passing laws to protect it. As of 2017, plastic bags were banned, and as of January 2019, plastic straws and cutlery and Styrofoam takeaway containers and plates were also legally banned. The use of sunscreen that contains oxybenzone—very harmful to the coral reefs—is also against the law.

Aruba with Kids

Aruba has a kid-loving culture, and its slogan "One Happy Island" extends to young visitors as well. The island is a reasonably short flight away from most of the Eastern Seaboard (about three to six hours). Though the island may not offer all of the distractions of a theme-park holiday, it has more than enough to keep most kids occupied during a family vacation.

WHERE TO STAY

Virtually all the best places for families to stay are on or along the beaches that run the length of the western side of the island. An ocean view isn't a necessity, but ease of access to one of the beaches is recommended.

Best High-Rise Resorts. High-rise resorts have a variety of amenities and activities; most offer kids' programs or dedicated kids' clubs. The Hyatt Regency Aruba Beach Resort offers an extensive kids' program and many family-fun activities, and the Ritz-Carlton Aruba has the Ritz Kidz program with seriously creative activities inspired by Jean-Michel Cousteau (Jacques Cousteau's son) and his Ocean Futures Society. Holiday Inn Resort Aruba has a great dedicated kids' club and a family fun zone, too.

Best Low-Rise Resorts. Mostly found along Eagle Beach, Manchebo Beach, and Druif Beach, low-rise resorts are often less crowded and offer fewer amenities and water sports than the high-rises, but they provide a relaxing, laid-back vibe, and some do have kids' programs. Amsterdam Manor on Eagle Beach is a good-value hotel with kitchenettes and a mini–grocery store on-site. At Divi and Tamarijn Aruba All-Inclusives on Druif Beach, children under 12 stay free when accompanied by two adults, and there's a kids' camp. Divi Dutch Village offers spacious suites with full kitchens and laundry facilities, and all nonmotorized water sports are included in the price. The Divi resorts also have a 30-foot-tall climbing tower on the beach.

BEACHES

Palm Beach is wide and offers powdery white sand, very calm waters, and plenty of nearby amenities like food and beverages. Families that want to avoid the crowds might find Druif and Manchebo beaches more to their liking, but there aren't many options for chair rentals though there is a public beach bar/restaurant now. Sprawling Eagle Beach has fewer crowds and a large range of amenities within easy

walking distance, but surf can be rough at times and the current strong, so take care with little ones there. Just outside of San Nicolas, Baby Beach—aptly named for its kid-friendly surf and protected pool of shallows waters—is worth a day away from the resorts.

WATER ACTIVITIES

Snorkeling, swimming, kayaking, and sailing are some of the things that keep families coming back to Aruba. Most hotels and condos offer inexpensive equipment rentals for a day in the water. Seasoned junior snorkelers will find the viewing pretty dull off the major beaches, so organized tours such as those offered by De Palm Tours and Red Sail Sports, and Jolly Pirates, which explores more remote coves, may provide a better underwater experience, plus they all stop at the massive Antilla Wreck in shallow water so kids can see it without diving. De Palm Island offers a variety of water activities for kids, including snorkeling and a water park that makes for a great day in the sun. The Atlantis Submarine Tour is also an ideal way to introduce children to Aruba's magical underwater world without getting them wet!

LAND ACTIVITIES

The **Aruba Ostrich Farm** is a short excursion, while **Philip's Animal Garden** is where kids will be entertained for hours by its many fun creatures and a huge playground. **The Butterfly Farm** is also a lovely experience for all ages, and if you go early in your holiday, you can return for free as many times as you want with your original admission voucher. **The Donkey Sanctuary Aruba** is also a must-visit. (Bring apples and carrots!)*And for evening activities, Paseo Herencia has a gorgeous waltzing waters show three times a night in their amphitheater–courtyard, and a carousel and small train. The massive new IMAX complex called Gloria also has a children's bouncy playground and a big food court.*

More adventurous families can try a day of hiking or explore the wild terrain by guided jeep safari tours or horseback, at **Arikok National Park;** don't miss climbing the other-worldly Casibari Rock Formations. In the Ayo area, a new glassblowing exhibition and café called Studio Murano Art teaches art through workshops and kids can make their own unique souvenirs. (Reservations needed.)

Understanding Local Eats

Arubans like their food spicy, and that's where the island's famous Madame Janette sauce comes in handy. It's made with Scotch bonnet peppers (similar to habanero peppers), which are so hot, they can burn your skin when they're broken open. Whether they're turned into *pika,* a relishlike mixture made with papaya, or sliced thin into vinegar and onions, these peppers are sure to set your mouth ablaze. Throw even a modest amount of Madame Janette sauce into a huge pot of soup, and your taste buds will tingle. (Referring to the sauce's spicy nature, Aruban men often refer to an attractive woman as a "Madame Janette.")

■TIP➔ **To tame the flames, don't go for a glass of water, as capsaicin, the compound in peppers that produces the heat, isn't water soluble. Dairy products (especially), sweet fruits, and starchy foods such as rice and bread are the best remedies.**

If you're interested in tasting other food that's unique to the Dutch- and Caribbean-influenced island, then you ought to try one of these local treats.

Balashi: After a day at the beach there's nothing better than sipping a nice, cold Balashi, Aruba's national beer and the only beer brewed on the island. The taste of Balashi is comparable to a Dutch pilsner.

Bitterballen: Crispy bite-size meatballs, which are breaded and then deep-fried, make for the perfect savory snack or appetizer. Dip them in a side of mustard, and wash them down with a cold beverage.

Cocada: Bite-size pieces of these sweet coconut candies are typically served on a coconut shell.

Funchi: This classic Aruban cornmeal side dish is eaten at all times of day and is commonly served with soup.

Keshi Yena: A traditional Aruban dish made with chicken, beef, or seafood in a rich brown sauce of spices and raisins, keshi yena is served with rice in a hollowed-out Gouda cheese rind.

Kesio: This popular dessert is essentially a custard flan or crème caramel.

Pan Bati: The slightly sweet pancakes are commonly eaten as a side with meat, fish, or soup entrées.

Pan Dushi: Delectable little raisin bread rolls are *dushi,* which is Papiamento for "sweet."

Pastechi: Aruba's favorite fast food is an empanadalike fried pastry filled with spiced meat, fish, or cheese.

Carnival

From New Year's Day to the first week in March, Aruba offers its biggest cultural celebration, incorporating local traditions with those of Venezuela, Brazil, Holland, and North America. Trinidadians who came to work at the oil refinery in the 1940s introduced Carnival and steel-pan music to the island; the instruments were originally made from old oil drums.

The monthlong celebration swings between downtown Oranjestad and the new Carnival Village in San Nicolas with pageants, parades, musical competitions, ceremonies, and gala concerts. Local dressmakers turn out the best costumes for parade days as well as the annual carnival queen competition and pageants.

Locals look forward to the Lighting Parade, a nighttime parade held in February that lights up the streets. The weeks in between, Aruba has many street parades, locally called "jump-ups," that lead up to the major parade in early March, including San Nicolas's Jouvert Morning Jump-Up (also called the Pajama Party, since it begins at 4 am and many people come straight from bed). The Grand Parade, as it is called, is held on the Sunday before Ash Wednesday for two days, first in San Nicolas and then in the capital city, Oranjestad, with thousands dancing in the streets and viewing the floats, costumes, and bands; it's the largest and longest carnival parade held on the ABC islands. All events end on Shrove Tuesday: at midnight an effigy of King Momo (traditionally depicted as a fat man) is burned to signal the end of the season. For event schedules visit www.aruba.com/us/calendar/aruba-carnival.

Aruba Shopping 101

Of course, there are typical souvenir choices in Aruba like baseball caps, refrigerator magnets, T-shirts, and key chains, but if you take the time to look, you can find items that were made on Aruba. Seek out the **Local Market** near the cruise ship terminal for great take-home items made by island artists and crafters.

■ TIP→ **It's not the string of flea market vendors along the marina; it's a stand-alone area of tents just across from the cruise terminal. Look for the big red chair.**

LOCAL ARTS AND CRAFTS

For high-quality arts and crafts made by local artisans, head to Cosecha Oranjestad (www.arubacosecha.com), housed in a big yellow building Downtown, or its sister organization, Cosecha San Nicolas. Products featured in Cosecha have been given the SEYO national seal of craftsmanship; the San Nicolas outlet hosts art and craft workshops as well. The Renaissance Marketplace holds a local arts and crafts market every Friday night from 7–10 pm; Paseo Herencia courtyard has a market Tuesday and Thursday nights; and the Ostrich Farm monthly farmers' markets. ArtAnCraft Aruba posts local artisans' events on their Facebook page (www.facebook.com/artandcraftaruba).

ECO-CONSCIOUS SOUVENIRS

Aruba outlawed plastic shopping bags in 2017. If you need a bag to carry your treasures, look for Arubiano (⊕ *arubiano.com*) grocery bags that feature iconic Aruban scenes shot by internationally known local photographer, Damilice Mansur; the company also sells flip-flops and hats with Aruba scenes on them. Not only are the bags made from recycled content, but part of the proceeds are donated to the local Aruba Birdlife Conservation foundation.

SHOPPING THAT GIVES BACK

American expat Jodi Tobman moved to Aruba in the 1990s and opened a chain of unique retail stores including The Juggling Fish (www.arubaswimwear.com), The Lazy Lizard (www.thelazylizard.com), and T.H. Palm and Co. (www.thpalmandcompany.com), which can be found in both the high-rise and low-rise hotel sectors. Tobman travels the globe seeking out unique products to stock the stores with—items like home goods, clothing, and jewelry, always with an eye toward handcrafted or sustainable or arty concepts. But most importantly, these stores are part of a community give-back program called Tikkun Olam—loosely translated as "repair

the world" in Hebrew—which donates a percentage of every purchase made in its stores to a local nonprofit of the buyer's choice.

A SPECIAL LOCAL PRODUCT

This happy island produces some of the world's finest aloe, and it's home to the world's oldest aloe company. Founded in 1890, **Aruba Aloe Balm N.V.** (arubaaloe.com) was one of the first companies to create and produce aloe-based skin-, hair-, and sun-care products. There are shops at the airport and all over the island and many of them have free samples so you can try their products made from Aruba's most prized natural resource.

Did You Know?

The beaches on Aruba are legendary: the solid seven miles of beachfront along its west coast are baby-powder soft, blindingly white sand carpets that smile over vsat expanses of clear azure water.

TRAVEL SMART

Updated by
Susan Campbell

★ **CAPITAL:**
Oranjestad

👤 **POPULATION:**
29,000

💬 **LANGUAGE:**
Dutch, Papiamento

$ **CURRENCY:**
Aruban florin (AWG)

☎ **COUNTRY CODE:**
297

⚠ **EMERGENCIES:**
911

🚗 **DRIVING:**
On the right

⚡ **ELECTRICITY:**
110 volts (same as U.S.)

🕐 **TIME:**
Atlantic Standard Time (same as the East Coast)

🌐 **WEBSITES:**
www.aruba.com

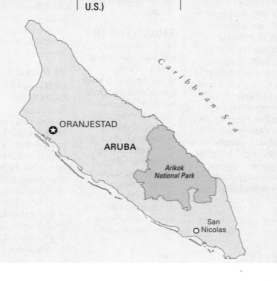

Know Before You Go

Should you tip in Aruba? If so, to whom and how much? Can you drink the water? Do people speak English or Dutch? Can you use American money, or should you exchange money? Does the island get hurricanes? We've got answers and a few tips to help you make the most of your visit.

WHAT'S THE WEATHER LIKE?

Aruba doesn't really have a rainy season and it's outside of the hurricane belt—one reason why the island is more popular than most during the off-season from mid-May through mid-November, when the risk of Atlantic hurricanes is at its highest. Temperatures are constant (along with the trade winds) year-round. Expect daytime temperatures in the 80s Fahrenheit and nighttime temperatures in the high 70s. Trade winds blow constantly at an average of 20 knots.

DO AMERICANS NEED A PASSPORT OR VISA?

A valid passport is required to enter or reenter the United States from Aruba.

U.S. tourists do not need a visa to travel to Aruba.

SHOULD YOU TIP?

Most restaurants add a service charge of 15%. It's not necessary to tip once a service charge has been added to the bill, but sometimes that tip is shared between all staff. If the service is good, an additional tip of 10% is always appreciated. If no service charge is included on the final bill, then leave the customary tip of 15% to 20%.

DON'T EXPECT LUSH GREENERY

Aruba is not a lush tropical island, and there are no rain forests. In fact, the island only averages 20 inches of rainfall per year. Beyond the palms transplanted on Palm Beach, there's very little greenery. The interior is arid and desertlike, and cacti, aloe, and divi-divi trees are the few plants hardy enough to survive and thrive.

IT'S OKAY TO DRINK THE WATER

Aruba's drinking water is among the safest and best tasting in the world and it comes from desalinated seawater. The local beer is also made from desalinated seawater.

NEW GREEN LAWS AFFECT SHOPPING

Aruba has passed some very forward-thinking environmental laws in the last few years. Plastic bags, Styrofoam plates, and plastic straws have been banned, so bring your own reusable shopping bag or buy a souvenir one there.

U.S. DOLLARS ARE FINE

You probably won't need to change any money if you're coming from the United States. American currency is accepted everywhere in Aruba, though you might get some change back in local currency—the Aruban florin, also called the guilder—at smaller, out-of-the-way stores.

THERE'S LOTS TO DO AFTER DARK

Beyond offering idyllic fun-in-the-sun days on gorgeous beaches, Aruba is renowned for its vibrant nightlife and glitzy casinos, most within easy walking distance of each other. The legal drinking and gambling age is 18, though there are a few exceptions where over 21 is the rule.

YES, THERE IS TRAFFIC

Oranjestad traffic can be heavy during rush hour. Allow a bit of extra time if you're trying to get into town for a dinner reservation or need to get to the airport at an appointed time.

If you rent a car, expect to have some issues with the island's multitude of roundabouts until you get used to them.

EVERYONE SPEAKS ENGLISH

Most Arubans speak at least four languages—English, Spanish, Papiamento, and Dutch. With the odd exception of domestic staff from Latin America working in the large resorts, you'll have no problem finding someone who speaks English.

ADDRESSES ARE INFORMAL

"Informal" might best describe Aruban addresses. Sometimes the street designation is in English (as in J. E. Irausquin Boulevard), other times in Dutch (as in Wilhelminas-traat); sometimes it's not specified whether something is a boulevard or a *straat* (street) at all. Street numbers follow street names, and postal codes aren't used. In rural areas you might have to ask a local for directions—and be prepared for such instructions as

"Take a right at the market, then a left where you see the big divi-divi tree."

ECO-FRIENDLY SUNSCREEN IS A MUST

The sun is very strong, and the trade winds can trick you into thinking you're not getting burned, so sunscreen is a must. However, Aruba has also passed a law against sunscreen that contains the coral-harming chemical oxyben-zone, so check that yours does not, or buy some eco-friendly screen when on island.

EXPECT TO RETURN

Don't stress if you don't get to do everything you want. Chances are good you'll be back, as Aruba has the highest repeat visitor ratio in the entire Caribbean (65%).

Getting Here and Around

Aruba is a small island, so it's virtually impossible to get lost when exploring. Most activities take place in and around Oranjestad or in the two main hotel areas, which are designated as the "low-rise" and "high-rise" areas. Main roads on the island are generally excellent, but getting to some of the more secluded beaches or historic sites will involve driving on unpaved tracks. Though Aruba is typically a very arid island, there can be occasional periods of heavy rain, and it's best to avoid exploring the national park or other wilderness areas during these times, since roads can become flooded, and muddy conditions can make driving treacherous.

Air

Aruba is 2½ hours from Miami; 4½ hours from New York; 5 hours from Boston, Chicago, Atlanta, or Toronto. Smaller airlines connect the Dutch islands in the Caribbean, often using Aruba as a hub; it's a ¼- to ½-hour hop (depending on whether you take a prop or a jet plane) from Curaçao to Aruba.

AIRPORTS
The island's Queen Beatrix International Airport (AUA) has been revamped recently and is equipped with thorough security, lots of flight displays, and state-of-the-art baggage-handling systems, shopping, and food-and-drink emporiums. There's also airportwide free Wi-Fi and new VIP club lounges and services.

GROUND TRANSPORTATION
A taxi from the airport to most hotels takes about 20 minutes (traffic depending). It costs about $26 to hotels along Eagle Beach, $31 to the high-rise hotels on Palm Beach, and $21 to hotels downtown. You'll find a taxi stand right outside the baggage-claim area. Aruba taxis are not metered; they operate on a flat rate by destination.

FLIGHTS
Many airlines fly nonstop to Aruba from several cities in North America; connections are usually at a U.S. airport.

There are nonstop flights from Atlanta (Delta), Baltimore (Southwest), Boston (American, JetBlue, US Airways), Charlotte (American), Chicago (United), Fort Lauderdale (Spirit, JetBlue), Houston (Southwest, United), Miami (American, Aruba Airlines), Newark (United), Minneapolis (Delta), New York–JFK (American, Delta, JetBlue), New York–Newark (United), Orlando (Southwest), Philadelphia (American), and Washington, D.C.–Dulles (United). Seasonal nonstops

from major Canadian cities are available from WestJet and Air Canada and charter airlines like Sunwing.

Because of pre-U.S. customs clearance, you really need three hours before departure from Aruba's airport. Beyond typical check-in lines—unless you check-in online and have no bags to check—you must go through two separate security checks and two customs as well. The entire procedure takes a lot of time, so be there early. You can get through a lot faster if you pay for the First Class Experience Aruba service that fast tracks you through all the lines (except U.S. Customs) and offers you a VIP lounge stay before departure.

🚲 Bicycle

Since the construction of the island's paved Linear Park, which lines the coast from downtown Oranjestad to the airport, and now also stretches from Fishermen's Huts beach to Malmok, casual cycling has become a big deal on Aruba. There's a bike-sharing program, Green Bike, that makes it easy to hop on one, or you can rent electric bicycles at Aruba E-Bike Tours. Some resorts offer their guests complimentary coaster bikes to pedal around on as well.

Bus

Arubus N.V. is Aruba's public transportation company. Island buses are clean, well maintained, sometimes air-conditioned, and regularly scheduled; they provide a safe, economical way to travel along the resort beaches all the way to the downtown Oranjestad main terminal. They stop at almost all major resorts and are a great way to hop into town for groceries to bring back to your hotel without taking expensive taxis. They run until fairly late at night and later on weekends. If you plan to take multiple trips in one day, purchase a day pass for US$10 at the main terminal in downtown Oranjestad for unlimited access to all their routes. Drivers give change if you don't have the exact fare (no large bills, though) and accept U.S. currency (but give change in florins). A one-way fare is US$2.60, and you can buy a return (round-trip) to Oranjestad for $5. Return bus fares to San Nicolas and Baby Beach from downtown are $8. Get all the updated information on rates, schedules, and routes on their website because things change often.

Getting Here and Around

Car

Driving is on the right, just as in the United States. Most of Aruba's major attractions are fairly easy to find, and there are great maps all over the island to find out-of-the-way spots (mapping apps can also help). International traffic signs and Dutch-style traffic signals (with an extra light for a turning lane) can be confusing, though, if you're not used to them; use extreme caution, especially at intersections, until you grasp the rules of the road.

GASOLINE

Gas prices average a little more than $1.27 a liter (roughly a quarter of a gallon), which is reasonable by Caribbean standards but more expensive than in the United States. Stations are plentiful in and near Oranjestad, San Nicolas, and Santa Cruz, and near the major high-rise hotels on the west coast. All take cash, and most take major credit cards. Nevertheless, gas prices aren't posted prominently, since they're fixed and the same at all stations.

PARKING

Parking downtown can be a challenge, but there is Aruparking (pay to park) and free parking behind the Renaissance Marketplace. Arupark meters accept local and U.S. coins, and credit cards, but if you're going to park downtown frequently, it's best to get a rechargeable SmartCard or download the iParkMe app to pay. Smart Cards are available at most stores and car rental kiosks and can be topped up at Aruparking and Arubus (see Bus) stations.

RENTAL CARS

In Aruba you must meet the minimum age requirements of each rental service. (Budget, for example, requires drivers to be over 25; Avis, over 23). A credit card (with a sufficient line of credit available) or a cash deposit of $500 is required. Rates vary seasonally and are usually lower from local agencies, but shopping for bargains and reserving a car online is a good strategy regardless of which company you rent from. Insurance is available starting at about $10 per day. Most visitors pick up their rental car at the airport, where you'll find both local and international brands; most companies have offices right across the road from the airport exit, but there are branches all over the island, including at major resorts. Most companies offer free drop-off and pickup at your hotel if you aren't renting a car on arrival. You can ask the concierge of your hotel or the front desk to recommend a

local rental if you only want one for a day to tour the island. Opt for a four-wheel-drive vehicle if you plan to explore the outback and go off the beaten path.

RENTAL-CAR INSURANCE

Everyone who rents a car wonders whether the insurance that the rental companies offer is worth the expense. No one—including us—has a simple answer. If you own a car, your personal auto insurance may cover a rental to some degree, though not all policies protect you abroad; always read your policy's fine print. If you don't have auto insurance, then seriously consider buying the collision- or loss-damage waiver (CDW or LDW) from the car-rental company, which eliminates your liability for damage to the car. Some credit cards offer CDW coverage, but it's usually supplemental to your own insurance and rarely covers SUVs, minivans, or luxury models. If your coverage is secondary, you may still be liable for loss-of-use costs from the car-rental company. But no credit-card insurance is valid unless you use that card for *all* transactions, from reserving to paying the final bill. It's sometimes cheaper to buy insurance as part of your general travel-insurance policy.

ROADSIDE EMERGENCIES

Discuss with the rental agency what to do in the case of an emergency. Make sure you understand what your insurance covers and what it doesn't; let someone at your accommodations know where you're heading and when you plan to return. Keep emergency numbers with you, just in case. Because Aruba is such a small island, you should never panic if you have car trouble; it's likely you'll be within relatively easy walking distance of a populated area unless you're in the national park.

ROAD CONDITIONS

Aside from the major highways, some of the island's winding roads are poorly marked (although the situation is slowly improving). Keep an eye out for rocks and other debris when driving on remote roads. When in the countryside, also keep your eyes open for wild goats and donkeys that might wander onto the road.

RULES OF THE ROAD

Despite the laid-back ways of locals, when they get behind the steering wheel they often speed and take liberties with road rules, especially outside the more heavily traveled Oranjestad and hotel areas. Keep a watchful eye for passing cars and for vehicles coming out of side roads. Speed limits

Getting Here and Around

are rarely posted, but the maximum speed is 60 kph (40 mph) and 40 kph (25 mph) through settlements. Speed limits and the use of seat belts are enforced.

Taxi

You'll find taxis at the airport and also at all major resorts (ask if you need one to be called). You don't really hail cabs in Aruba; if you need one, just go to the nearest hotel, and the doorman will get you one. Your restaurant or bar will also call one for you. In downtown Oranjestad, taxis are always to be found around the Renaissance Marina lower lobby. Taxi rates in Aruba are fixed (i.e., there are no meters; the rates are set by the government and displayed on a chart by zone) and are posted on the Aruba Tourism Authority website and the Aruba airport website, though you should confirm the fare with your driver before your ride begins. Minimum fare is US$7. There is an additional $3 charge to regular fares from 11 pm to 7 am and on some holidays. Be forewarned that taxi drivers will not allow anyone in wet bathing suits or wet shorts in their vehicles.

Essentials

Activities

Since soft, sandy beaches and turquoise waters are the biggest draws in Aruba, they can be crowded. Eagle Beach is the less crowded of the main ones and the best the island has to offer for postcard-perfect scenery. Diving is also good in Aruba; there are many wrecks to explore.

Near-constant breezes and tranquil, protected waters have proven to be a boon for windsurfers and kiteboarders, who have discovered that conditions on the southwestern coast are ideal for their sport.

A largely undeveloped region in Arikok National Park is the destination of choice for visitors wishing to hike and explore some wild terrain.

Beaches

The beaches on Aruba are legendary: the solid 7 miles of beachfront along its west coast are baby-powder-soft, blindingly white sand carpets that smile over vast expanses of clear azure water with varying degrees of surf action. The waters of Palm Beach in front of the high-rise resort strip are typically pond-still placid, whereas the waves on the low-rise resort strip on

Eagle Beach are typically restless and rolling. The beaches on the northeastern side are unsafe for swimming because of strong currents and rough swells, but they are worth seeking out for their natural beauty and romantic vistas. You might see bodyboarders and kitesurfers out there, but they are typically highly skilled locals who know the conditions well. Swimming on the sunrise side of the island is best done in Savaneta at Mangel Halto and in San Nicolas at Rodger's Beach or Baby Beach, named for its toddler-friendly calm waters.

Dining

There are hundreds of restaurants on Aruba, from elegant eateries to seafront beach bars, and you can sample a wide range of cuisines reflecting Aruba's extensive blend of cultures; due to a large number of repeat tourists from the United States, American-style fare is everywhere. Chefs must be creative on this tiny island because of the limited number of locally grown ingredients—beyond fresh fish and seafood, much is imported—but lately, they are getting much better at providing farm-to-fork menus when possible and catering to restricted diets like gluten-free

Essentials

and vegan. In fact, Aruba has become one of the Caribbean's most vegan-friendly islands with many restaurants adding lots of creative and tasty plant-based options to their regular menus and even creating stand-alone vegan menus.

A return to local roots is also trending in the foodie scene; the new authentic Aruban lunch buffet at Elements proved to be so popular with locals and visitors alike that they also extended it to their dinner offerings. And catch-of-the-day including local lobster has little local eateries like Taste My Aruba really hopping with visitors every night. Fusions of styles and choices of cuisines all under one roof has also become a thing—the collection of dining spots at the new Cove Mall is like the United Nations, and the new Bochincha Container Yard venue offers eight different types of food kiosks as part of their appeal.

Breakfast lovers are in luck as most resorts have bountiful breakfast buffets, and you can't go wrong at Dutch Pancakehouse at any time of day. But it's a la carte brunches (and not only on Sundays) that have been popping up all over the place, some in expected spots like the luxury brunch at Senses chef's table, and

the monthly Friday brunch at Windows on Aruba.

Although most resorts offer better-than-average dining, ask locals about their favorite spots; some of the lesser-known restaurants, snacks, and food trucks offer excellent reasonably priced food worth sleuthing out. Most restaurants on the western side of the island are along Palm Beach or in downtown Oranjestad, both easily accessible by taxi or bus. Some restaurants in Savaneta and San Nicolas are worth the trip, too.

The island is also a particularly family-friendly destination, so bringing the kids along is rarely a problem, and many restaurants offer children's menus.

Unless otherwise noted, the restaurants listed in this guide are open daily for lunch and dinner.

ARUBAN CUISINE

Aruba shares many of its traditional foods with Bonaire and Curaçao. These dishes are a fusion of the various influences that have shaped the culture of the islands. Proximity to mainland South America means that many traditional snack and breakfast foods of Venezuelan origin, such as empanadas, have been adopted into local eats; on Aruba they are called *pastechis* and come with a

wide variety of fillings. The Dutch influence is evident in the fondness for cheese of all sorts, but especially Gouda. *Keshi yena,* ground meat or seafood with seasonings placed in a hollowed-out cheese rind before baking, is a national dish. Arubans also love their *bolos* (cakes), so look for local favorites like cashew nut, pistachio, or chocolate rum cake.

If there's one thread that unites the cuisines of the Caribbean, it's cornmeal, and Arubans love nothing more than a side of *funchi* (like a thick polenta) or a *pan bati* (a fried cornmeal pancake) to make a traditional meal complete. Though Aruban cuisine isn't by nature spicy, it's almost always accompanied by a small bowl of spicy *pica* (a condiment of fiery hot peppers and onions in vinegar) or a bottle of hot sauce made from local peppers. An abundance of fish means that seafood is the most popular protein on the island, and it's been said that if there were an Aruban national dish, it would be the catch of the day.

PRICES AND DRESS
Aruba's elegant restaurants—where you might have to dress up a little (jackets for men, sundresses for women)—can be pricey. If you want to spend fewer florins, opt for the more casual spots, where being comfortable is the only dress requirement. A sweater draped over your shoulders will go a long way against the chill of air-conditioning. If you plan to eat in the open air, bring along insect repellent in case the mosquitoes get unruly.

We assume that restaurants and hotels accept credit cards. If they don't, we'll note it in the review.

RESERVATIONS
To ensure that you get to eat at the restaurants of your choice, make some calls or visit the website when you get to the island—especially during high season—to secure reservations. Many restaurants now have online booking options. On Sunday you may have a hard time finding a restaurant that's open for lunch; some eateries are closed all day Monday.

We mention reservations only when they're essential (there's no other way you'll ever get a table, like at intimate Chef's Table venues) or when they're not accepted. We mention dress only when men are required to wear a jacket or a jacket and tie.

TIPPING
Most restaurants add a service charge of 15%. It's not necessary to tip once a service

Essentials

charge has been added to the bill, but sometimes that tip is shared between all staff. If the service is good, an additional tip of 10% is always appreciated. If no service charge is included on the final bill, then leave the customary tip of 15% to 20%.

WINES, BEER, AND SPIRITS

Arubans have a great love for wine, so even small supermarkets have a fairly good selection of European and South American wines at prices that are reasonable by Caribbean standards. The beer of choice in Aruba is the island-brewed Balashi and Balashi Chill often served with a wedge of lime. Local spirits also include *ponce crema,* a wickedly potent eggnog type of drink and *coecoei,* a thick, red-licorice-tasting liqueur that's an integral ingredient in the island's famous signature cocktail Aruba Ariba.

What It Costs in U.S. Dollars			
$	$$	$$$	$$$$
RESTAURANTS			
under $12	$12–$20	$21–$30	over $30
HOTELS			
under $275	$275–$375	$376–$475	over $475

Prices in the restaurant reviews are the average cost of a main course at dinner or,

if dinner isn't served, at lunch; taxes and service charges are generally included. Prices in the hotel reviews are the lowest cost of a standard double room in high season, excluding taxes, service charges, and meal plans (except at all-inclusives). Prices for rentals are the lowest per-night cost for a one-bedroom unit in high season.

 ## Embassy/Consulate

There is no U.S. embassy on Aruba. If you need assistance you must call the embassy in Curaçao.

● Health and Safety

Arubans are very friendly, so you needn't be afraid to stop and ask anyone for directions. It's a relatively safe island, but commonsense rules still apply. Lock your rental car when you leave it, and leave valuables in your hotel safe. Don't leave bags unattended in the airport, on the beach, or on tour vehicles.

As a rule, water is pure and food is wholesome in hotels and local restaurants throughout Aruba, but be cautious when buying food from street vendors. And just as you would at home, wash or peel all fruits

and vegetables before eating them. Traveler's diarrhea, caused by consuming contaminated water, unpasteurized milk and milk products, and unrefrigerated food, isn't a big problem—unless it happens to you. So watch what you eat, especially at outdoor buffets in the hot sun. Make sure cooked food is hot and cold food has been properly refrigerated.

The major health risk is sunburn or sunstroke. Use sunscreen with an SPF of at least 15—especially if you're fair—and apply it liberally on your nose, ears, and other sensitive and exposed areas. Make sure the sunscreen is water-resistant if you're engaging in water sports. Aruba has a law that sunscreen must be reef-friendly, so if you cannot find a suitable brand at home you can buy it on island.

Always limit your sun time for the first few days, and drink plenty of liquids. Limit intake of caffeine and alcohol, which hasten dehydration.

Mosquitoes can be bothersome if you are dining outside so pack (or buy on island) eco-friendly bug repellent. The strong trade winds generally keep them at bay during the day unless you are in thick foliage or mangrove areas near the water. It's at dusk that they come out, when winds

calm, and at night when you are dining with toes in the sand. Zika and dengue have been reported on Aruba, but the island is not considered a high-risk zone. Protect yourself regardless.

Don't fly within 24 hours of scuba diving. In an emergency, Air Ambulance service will fly you to Curaçao at a low altitude if you need to get to a decompression chamber.

IMMUNIZATIONS

Although COVID-19 brought travel to a virtual standstill for most of 2020 and into 2021, vaccinations have made travel possible and safe again. Remaining requirements and restrictions—including those for non-vaccinated travelers—can, however, vary from one place (or even business) to the next. Check out the websites of the CDC and the U.S. Department of State, both of which have destination-specific, COVID-19 guidance. Also, in case travel is curtailed abruptly again, consider buying trip insurance. Just be sure to read the fine print: not all travel-insurance policies cover pandemic-related cancellations. Keep up to date on Aruba's traveler's health requirements at their official website (www.aruba.com/us/traveler-health-requirements).

Essentials

OVER-THE-COUNTER REMEDIES

There are a number of pharmacies and stores selling medications throughout the island (including at most hotels), and virtually anything obtainable in North America is available in Aruba. There is also a walk-in doctor's clinic at Botica di Servicio on the Palm Beach strip.

RESTROOMS

Outside Oranjestad, the public restrooms can be found in small restaurants that dot the countryside.

Internet

Resort-wide free Wi-Fi is common in Aruba. Almost all Aruba resort hotels offer it and many bars and dining spots and even stores also offer free Wi-Fi; just ask them for their password when you order or buy something. There are also free government-sponsored Wi-Fi hot spots and zones for tourists and locals with more to come. Just remember, public networks are not secure.

Lodging

Aruba is known for its large, luxurious high-rise resorts and vast array of time-shares. But the island also has a nice selection of smaller, low-rise resorts for travelers who don't want to feel lost in a large, impersonal hotel complex. If you're on a budget, consider booking one of the island's many apartment-style units, so you can eat in sometimes instead of having to rely on restaurants exclusively. Aruba also has Airbnb now, too.

Most Aruba hotels are found in two clusters: the low-rise hotels in a stretch along Druif Beach and Eagle Beach, and the high-rise hotels on a stretch of Palm Beach. With a few exceptions, the hotels in the high-rise area tend to be larger and more expensive than their low-rise counterparts, but they usually offer a wider range of services.

Accommodations in Aruba run the gamut from large high-rise hotels and resorts to sprawling condo complexes to small, locally owned boutique establishments, and even luxury villa rentals in well-designed private communities where fractional ownership is also an option. Most hotels are west of Oranjestad, along L. G. Smith and J. E. Irausquin Boulevards. Many are self-contained complexes, with restaurants, shops, casinos, water-sport centers, health clubs, and spas. And there are a surprising number of small and economical apartment-style

hotels, bed-and-breakfasts, and family-run escapes in the interior if you know where to look. The number of all-inclusive options is growing, and increasingly, big-name-brand hotels are beginning to offer more comprehensive meal plan options. Savaneta now offers South Pacific over-the-water-style bungalows at Aruba Ocean Villas, as well as treehouse stays. Time-shares have always been big on this island, and the Divi family of resorts offers many different options in their various locations.

Large Resorts: These all-encompassing vacation destinations offer myriad dining options, casinos, shops, water-sports centers, health clubs, and car-rental desks. The island also has many all-inclusive options.

Time-Shares: Large time-share properties are also popular, luring visitors who prefer to prepare some of their own meals and have a bit more living space than you might find in the typical resort hotel room plus fully stocked kitchens with everything you need for cooking … except the food. You can order your groceries online to be stocked ahead at many resorts now, too.

Boutique Resorts: You'll find a few small resorts that offer more personal service, and better reflect the natural sense of Aruban hospitality you'll find all over the island. There are some lovely B&Bs as well.

■ TIP→ **Hotels have private bathrooms, phones, and TVs, and don't offer meals unless we specify a meal plan in the review (i.e., breakfast, some meals, all meals, all-inclusive). We always list facilities but not whether you'll be charged an extra fee to use them.**

APARTMENT AND HOUSE RENTALS

Apartments and time-share condos are common in Aruba. So if you're looking for more space for your family or group to spread out in (and especially if you want to have access to a kitchen to make some meals), this can be a very budget-friendly option. The money you save can be used for more dining and activities. Many time-share resorts are full service, offering the same range of water sports and other activities as any other resort, and almost all of them offer unused units on their websites (some through third-party booking sites). And some regular resorts also have a time-share component. Airbnb also offers rental options on the island ranging from tiny cottage-style stays to luxurious stand-alone villas.

Essentials

RESERVATIONS

When making reservations, be sure you understand how much you are really paying before finalizing any reservation. Hotels collect 9.5% in taxes, which goes to marketing to tourists, and $0.50 per room night (which goes to marketing to tourists). An additional $3 Environment Levy per day was added in 2013. Service charge is dependent on the hotel.

Some resorts will allow you to cancel without any kind of penalty—even if you prepaid to secure a discounted rate—if you cancel at least 24 hours in advance. Others require you to cancel a week in advance or penalize you the cost of one night. Small inns and B&Bs are most likely to require you to cancel far in advance. Most hotels allow children under a certain age to stay in their parents' room at no extra charge, but others charge for them as extra adults; find out the cutoff age for discounts.

$ Money

Arubans happily accept U.S. dollars virtually everywhere, so most travelers will find no real need to exchange money. The official currency is the Aruban florin (Afl), also called the guilder, which is made up of 100 cents. Silver coins come in denominations of 1, 2½, 5, 10, 25, and 50 (the square one) cents. Paper currency comes in denominations of 5, 10, 25, 50, and 100 florins.

Prices quoted throughout this book are in U.S. dollars unless otherwise noted.

For purchases you'll pay a 1.5% BBO tax (a turnover tax on each level of sale for all goods and services) in all but the duty-free shops.

Prices throughout this guide are given for adults. Substantially reduced fees are almost always available for children, students, and seniors.

ATMS AND BANKS

If you need fast cash, you'll find ATMs that accept international cards (and dispense cash in both U.S. and local currency) at banks in Oranjestad, at the major malls, and along the roads leading to the hotel strip, as well as in every casino and at the airport.

Y Nightlife

Aruba comes alive by night, and has become a true party hot spot. The casinos—though not as elaborate as those in Las Vegas—are among the best of any Caribbean island.

For information on specific events, check out the free

magazines and island guides you can get at the airport and in hotel lobbies.

📷 Packing

Dress on Aruba is generally casual. Bring loose-fitting clothing made of natural fabrics to see you through days of heat and humidity. Pack a beach cover-up, both to protect yourself from the sun and to provide something to wear to and from your hotel room. Bathing suits and immodest attire are frowned upon away from the beach. A sun hat is advisable, but you don't have to pack one—inexpensive straw hats are available everywhere—but be forewarned that the wind is constant so you might have to tie it or find a firm fitting one. For shopping and sightseeing, bring shorts, jeans, T-shirts, cotton shirts, slacks, sundresses, and good walking shoes. Nighttime dress can range from very informal to casually elegant, depending on the establishment. A tie is practically never required, but a jacket may be appropriate in fancy restaurants. You may need a light sweater or jacket for evening especially when dining indoors as the air-conditioning can be set very high in many restaurants.

🆕 Performing Arts

Aruba has a handful of not-so-famous but very talented performers. Over the years, several local artists, including composer Julio Renado Euson, choreographer Wilma Kuiperi, sculptor Ciro Abath, and visual artist Elvis Lopez, have gained international renown. Furthermore, many Aruban musicians play more than one type of music (classical, jazz, soca, salsa, reggae, calypso, rap, pop), and many compose as well as perform. Edjean Semeleer has followed in the footsteps of his mentor Padu Lampe—the composer of the island's national anthem and a beloved local star—to become one of the island's best-loved entertainers. His performances pack Aruba's biggest halls, especially his annual Christmas concert. He sings in many languages, and though he's young, his style is old-style crooner—Aruba's answer to Michael Bublé. The past few years have seen a new crop of young rap and hip-hop artists also out to make their mark as well.

Essentials

☎ Phones

To call Aruba direct from the United States, dial 011–297, followed by the seven-digit number in Aruba.

LOCAL CALLS
Dial the seven-digit number.

CALLING THE UNITED STATES
Dial 0, then 1, the area code, and the number. AT&T customers can dial 800–8000 from special phones at the cruise dock and in the airport's arrival and departure halls and charge calls to their credit card.

MOBILE PHONES
Both SETAR and Digicel offer rental phones, but if you are staying for more than a week, it may be just as cost-effective to buy a cheap phone; even easier is buying a prepaid local SIM and using it in your own unlocked phone. Most U.S.–based GSM and CDMA cell phones work on Aruba.

If you have a multiband phone (some countries use frequencies different from those used in the United States) and your service provider uses the world-standard GSM network (as do T-Mobile, AT&T, and Verizon), you can probably use your phone abroad. Roaming fees can be steep. And overseas you normally pay the toll charges for incoming calls. It's almost always cheaper to send a text message than to make a call.

■ TIP→ **Take advantage of the island's abundant free Wi-Fi and use Internet-based apps for making calls like Google Hangouts and WhatsApp.**

📦 Shipping

Post Aruba's website has all the information you need for sending mail. From Aruba to the United States or Canada a letter costs Afl2.20 (about $1.25) and a postcard costs Afl1.30 (75¢). Expect it to take one to two weeks. When addressing letters to Aruba, don't worry about the lack of formal addresses or postal codes; the island's postal service knows where to go.

If you need to send a package in a hurry, there are a few options. FedEx offers overnight service to the United States if you get your package in before 3 pm; there is a convenient office in downtown Oranjestad. Another big courier service is UPS, and several smaller local courier services, most of them open weekdays 9 to 5, also provide international deliveries.

🛍 Shopping

Shopping can be good on Aruba. Although stores on the island often use the tagline "duty-free," the word "prices" is usually printed underneath in much smaller letters. The only real duty-free shopping is in the departures area of the airport. (Passengers bound for the United States should be sure to shop before proceeding through U.S. customs in Aruba.) Downtown stores do have very low sales tax, though, and they offer some excellent bargains on high-end luxury items like gold, silver, gems, and high-end watches. Major credit cards are welcome everywhere, as are U.S. dollars.

A good way to preview the shops and malls in downtown Oranjestad is to hop aboard the free trolley that loops the downtown area. There are some interesting new offerings in the backstreets, including big name-brand megastores wedged in between smaller mom-and-pop shops. Also the smaller malls along the strip like the Village Square have some unique artisan shops, as does Paseo Herencia, whose courtyard is the scene of nightly entertainment called "the Waltzing Waters."

Aruba's souvenir and crafts stores are full of delft Dutch porcelains and figurines, as befits the island's heritage. Dutch cheese is a good buy, as are hand-embroidered linens and any products made from the native aloe vera plant— sunburn cream, face masks, or skin refreshers found in the many official Aruba Aloe stores; new eco-friendly sunscreen mandated by law is also available. Local arts and crafts run toward wood carvings and earthenware emblazoned with "Aruba: One Happy Island" and the like, but there are many shops with unique Aruban items like designer wear and fancy flip-flops and artwork if you know where to look. And arts foundations like Cosecha in Oranjestad and San Nicolas offer up only certifiably authentic, high-quality arts and crafts made in Aruba by talented local artisans. Don't try to bargain unless you are at a flea market or stall. Arubans consider it rude to haggle, despite what you may hear to the contrary.

There is late-night shopping in two locations. The first, in downtown Oranjestad at Renaissance Mall—a multilevel indoor-outdoor complex—stays open until 8 pm, and shops in the modern, multilevel indoor shopping mall off the high-rise strip—Palm Beach Plaza—stay open until 10 pm. Many of the shops around Paseo Herencia also stay open late in high

Essentials

season. A few other shops that stay open late can be found in Alhambra Mall as well. And most resorts have their own shops, but don't expect plastic bags for your goods or groceries, as Aruba banned them in 2017. There are really nice reusable bags for purchase all over the place that are made from recycled materials, and some of them are imprinted with authentic Aruba scenes that make great souvenirs as well.

⦿ Visitor Information

CUSTOMS AND DUTIES

Travelers to the United States clear Customs and Immigration before leaving Aruba. You can bring up to 1 liter of spirits, 3 liters of beer, or 2.25 liters of wine per person, and up to 200 cigarettes or 50 cigars into Aruba. You don't need to declare the value of gifts or other items, although customs officials may inquire about large items or large quantities of goods and charge (at their discretion) an import tax of 7.5% to 22% on items worth more than $230. Meat, birds, and illegal substances are forbidden. You may be asked to provide written verification that plants are free of diseases. If you're traveling with pets,

bring a veterinarian's note attesting to their good health.

HOLIDAYS

Aruba's official holidays are New Year's Day, Good Friday, Easter Sunday, and Christmas, as well as Betico Croes Day (January 25), National Anthem and Flag Day (March 18), King's Day (April 30), Labor Day (May 1), and Ascension Day (39 days after Easter).

WEDDINGS

People over the age of 18 can marry as long as they submit the appropriate documents 14 days in advance. Couples are required to submit birth certificates with raised seals, through the mail or in person, to Aruba's Office of the Civil Registry. They also need an apostil—a document proving they're free to marry—from their country of residence. Same-sex ceremonies are available on Aruba, though they're not legally binding.

With so many beautiful spots to choose from, weddings on Aruba are guaranteed to be romantic. Most resorts have their own wedding planning department or use a local partner and they can handle everything from start to finish for you. Aruba also now hosts the world's largest vow renewal group ceremony for couples from all over the world on Eagle Beach each year.

 When to Go

Aruba's high season runs from early December through mid-April. During this season you're guaranteed the most entertainment at resorts and the most people with whom to enjoy it. January and February are the most expensive times to visit, both for people staying a week or more and for cruise-ship passengers coming ashore. During this period hotels are solidly booked, and you must make reservations at least two or three months in advance for the very best places (and to get the best airfares). During the rest of the year hotel prices can drop 20% to 40% after April 15.

Contacts

Air

CONTACTS Sunwing Airlines.
✉ Toronto ☎ 800/877–1755
🌐 www.sunwing.ca. **Westjet.**
✉ Toronto ☎ 888/937–8538
🌐 www.westjet.com. **First Class Aruba.** ✉ Queen Beatrix International Airport, Sabana Berde, Oranjestad 🌐 www.firstclassaruba.com.

Bicycle

CONTACTS Aruba E-Bike Tours.
✉ Oranjestad ☎ 297/592–5550
🌐 www.arubaebiketours.com. **Aruba Motorcycle Tours.**
✉ Oranjestad ☎ 297/641–7818
🌐 arubamotorcycletours.com. **Green Bike Aruba.** ✉ Oranjestad ☎ 297/594–6368 🌐 greenbikearuba.com.

Bus

CONTACTS Arubus. ✉ Oranjestad 🌐 www.arubus.com.

Car

CAR RENTALS Amigo. ✉ Across from Arrival Terminal Airport and in Oranjestad, Schotlandstraat 56 ☎ 297/583–8833
🌐 www.amigocar.com.
Avis. ✉ Reina Beatrix Airport ☎ 297/582–5496 in Aruba, 800/532–1527 🌐 www.avis.

com. **Budget.** ✉ Reina Beatrix Airport ☎ 297/582–8600, 800/472–3325 in Aruba 🌐 www.budgetaruba.com.
Thrifty. ✉ Reina Beatrix Airport ☎ 297/583–4902 🌐 www.thriftycarrentalaruba.com.
Tropic Car Rental. ✉ Reina Beatrix Airport ☎ 297/583–7336
🌐 www.tropiccarrent-aruba.com.

PARKING Aruparking. ✉ Oranjestad 🌐 www.aruparking.com.

Embassy/Consulate

CONTACTS U.S. Consulate Curaçao. ✉ J.B. Gorsiraweg 1, Willemstad ☎ 9/461–3066
🌐 cw.usconsulate.gov.

Phones

CONTACTS Digicel. ✉ Oranjestad ☎ 297/522–2222
🌐 www.digicelaruba.com. **SETAR.** ✉ Oranjestad ☎ 297/525–1000 🌐 www.setar.aw.

Taxi

CONTACTS Arubas Transfer Tour & Taxi C.A. ✉ Reina Beatrix Airport ☎ 297/582–2116, 297/582–2010 🌐 www.airportaruba.com/taxi-transportation.

📍 Visitor Information

CONTACTS Aruba Food and Beverage Association. ✉ *Oranjestad* ☎ *297/280–1312* ⊕ *www.arubadining.com.* **Aruba Hotel & Tourism Association.** ✉ *Oranjestad* ☎ *297/582–2607* ⊕ *www.ahata.com.* **Aruba Tourism Authority.** ✉ *L. G. Smith Blvd. 8, Oranjestad* ☎ *800/862–7822 in the U.S./ international, 297/582–3777 in Aruba* ⊕ *www.aruba.com.*
Papiamento Online Courses. ✉ *Oranjestad* ⊕ *https://cudoo. com/product-category/languages/papiamento.*
Post Aruba. ✉ *Oranjestad* ⊕ *www.postaruba.com.*

WEDDINGS Aruba Fairy Tales Weddings. ✉ *Costa Linda Beach Resort, Oranjestad* ☎ *297/593–0045* ⊕ *arubafairytales. com.* **Aruba Weddings for You.** ✉ *Oranjestad* ☎ *297/525–5293* ⊕ *www.arubaweddingsforyou. com.* **Dream Weddings Aruba.** ✉ *Matadera 9W, Noord* ☎ *297/587–5991* ⊕ *www. dreamweddingsaruba.com.*

Papiamento Primer

Papiamento is a hybrid language born out of the colorful past of Aruba, Bonaire, and Curaçao. The language's use is generally thought to have started in the 17th century when Sephardic Jews migrated with their African slaves from Brazil to Curaçao. The slaves spoke a pidgin Portuguese, which may have been blended with pure Portuguese, some Dutch (the colonial power in charge of the island), and Arawakan. Proximity to the mainland meant that Spanish and English words were also incorporated.

Papiamento is roughly translated as "the way of speaking." (Sometimes the suffix -mentu is spelled in the Spanish and Portuguese way -mento, creating the variant spelling.) It began as an oral tradition, handed down through the generations and spoken by all social classes on the islands. There's no uniform spelling or grammar from island to island, or even from one neighborhood to another. Nevertheless, it's beginning to receive some official recognition, and anyone applying for citizenship must be fluent in both Papiamento and Dutch.

Arubans enjoy it when visitors use their language, so don't be shy. You can buy a Papiamento dictionary to build your vocabulary, and there are online courses and videos to help you as well, but here are a few pleasantries to get you started:

Bon dia. Good morning.

Bon tardi. Good afternoon.

Bon nochi. Good evening/night.

Bon bini. Welcome.

Ayo. Bye.

Te aworo. See you later.

Pasa un bon dia. Have a good day.

Danki. Thank you.

Na bo ordo. You're welcome.

Con ta bai? How are you?

Mi ta bon. I am fine.

Ban goza! Let's enjoy!

Pabien! Congratulations!

Quanto costa esaki? How much is this?

Hopi bon. Very good.

Ami. Me.

Abo. You.

Nos dos. The two of us.

Mi dushi. My sweetheart.

Dushi. Sweet or cool.

Ku tur mi amor. With all my love.

Un braza. A hug.

Un sunchi. A kiss.

Mi stima Aruba. I love Aruba.

How to Spend 5 Days in Aruba

If you're heading to One Happy Island, you probably intend to spend a lot at time on the beach, but there are some excellent reasons to roll out of that surf-side hammock and explore more of Aruba, some of which include some quality time in the sea. But don't worry, all of Aruba's beaches are public, so you can take a dip wherever you like.

DAY 1: PALM BEACH PLEASURES

Even if you're staying elsewhere, **Palm Beach** is worth a visit on your first day to see where all the action is. Make sure you come in your bathing suit (with a change of clothes) because this area is famous for its water sports and sailing and snorkel excursions, as well as its dining, shopping, and nightlife options. It's safe to walk day or night, and compact enough to discover on foot. Visit the **Butterfly Farm Aruba** while there: the visit takes about an hour or so, and your initial admission is good for repeat visits … just in case. Plan for lunch at one of the many beachfront cafés, take-outs, or pier bars.

After dark, don't miss the colorful free nightly water shows at **Paseo Herencia,** and the new cornucopia of nightlife and dining at **The Cove Mall** including the new rooftop hot

spot, **The Vue.** If you're heading north on the strip towards the **Aruba Marriott Resort** or its **Stellaris Casino,** dinner at **Atardi** is a good bet, especially if you're looking for toes-in-the-sand dining.

LOGISTICS

Accessible by public bus or taxi, or simply drive along Route 1B, which runs along the coast from tip to tip. (1A is northbound, 1B is southbound.)

DAY 2: DOWNTOWN DELIGHTS

You can spend an entire day discovering downtown **Oranjestad's** colorful mélange of local eateries, shops, historic buildings, museums, and refurbished main street arcades and courtyards. It's an easily walkable grid, but if you don't feel like walking, you can hop on and off the free **Downtown Trolley** or join a guided outing with **Aruba Walking Tours.** If you're hot after shopping, head to the urban oasis known as **Surfside Beach Bar,** less than a mile away to cool off on their lovely little beach or at **Reflexions**, the trendy seafront lounge next door. Enjoy a stellar sunset there, then head to the lively **Renaissance Marketplace** for casinos, alfresco dining, nightlife, and free live entertainment. Or check out the exciting new

How to Spend 5 Days in Aruba

night scene behind Renaissance Marine hotel and dine at alfresco at **Taste My Aruba** and go for nightcaps at the new hot spots like **Patio 15, Hoya Cocktail Bar,** or **The Umbrella Lounge**, all within easy walking distance from each other. (Just follow your ears, you'll hear their music.) Just outside of downtown proper is also the new **Bochincha Container Yard,** a massive alfresco dining and entertainment complex behind the Local Market.

LOGISTICS
Take Route 1B straight to downtown, take a taxi, or hop a public bus.

DAY 3: GO WILD
Rent a car or a private driver for the day and head southeast to discover the best locally caught fish and seafood meals at **Zeerovers** for lunch in **Savaneta,** and then head back to Route 1 to continue on to **San Nicolas** to see why it's called Aruba's answer to Miami's Wynwood area. The outdoor art is epic. If you want to know more about the art, join a jaunt with **Aruba Murals Tours.** Just don't forget your bathing suit, because you'll want to head on to **Baby Beach** for a dip and an hour or two of beach time. For refreshments, stop at **Rum Reef,** an adults-only infinity pool and bar, or the more casual **Big**

Mamma's family-friendly grill at the other end of the beach. Head back to Savaneta for dinner at **Flying Fishbone** or **The Old Man and the Sea,** but make sure you have a reservation well ahead for both.

LOGISTICS
You can drive there, but it's not recommended for first-timers. All tours include hotel pickup and drop-off, so sit back and let the adventure begin.

DAY 4: SLEUTH OUT SOUTHEAST COAST SURPRISES
Rent a car and head southeast to discover the best locally caught fish and seafood meals at **Zeerovers** for lunch in **Savaneta,** and then head back to Route 1 to continue on to **San Nicolas** to see why it's called Aruba's answer to Miami's Wynwood area. The outdoor art is epic. If you want to know more about the art, join a jaunt with **Aruba Murals Tours.** Just don't forget your bathing suit, because you'll want to head on to **Baby Beach** for a dip and an hour or two of beach time. Head back to Savaneta for dinner at **Flying Fishbone.**

■ TIP→ **Reserve ahead at Flying Fishbone if you want to dine with your feet in the water.**

LOGISTICS

For San Nicolas, follow Route 1A; for Savaneta, make a right turn at the Super S-Chows' Supermarket, follow the sign for Flying Fishbone. Get back on 1A for San Nicolas.

DAY 5: YOUR LAST DAY

Flights usually leave in the late afternoon; spend an hour or so at the beach before heading to the airport. Make sure to leave plenty of time at the airport, as there are about seven steps that involve picking up and dropping your luggage numerous times before you clear Customs and can head to the waiting areas. The airport now has a VIP lounge, accessible if you have a Priority Pass membership or spring for the extra cost of being ushered through all the lines like a celebrity (except for U.S. customs) with **First Class Aruba**.

If not, you can always go have a last tropical cocktail in "The Crying Room," a small corner of the airport's **One Happy Bar,** aptly named as it's famous for inducing the tears of those who always hate to leave Aruba. (Be forewarned they have a sign that limits crying to 15 minutes.)

WHAT IF IT RAINS?

Even though Aruba is outside the hurricane belt, you may find yourself with the rare rainy day, or you might just want a break from the tropical heat if you overdid the sunbathing. That's a perfect time to explore some indoor attractions like the free **Museum of Archelogy** in downtown Oranjestad and ride the free ecotrolley around the newly refreshed Main Street and see what's on offer. There are lots of souvenir and high-end shopping options there, or you can head to the modern, multilevel Palm Beach Plaza for all kinds of shopping and entertainment like bowling. Or check out the massive new stand-alone IMAX cinema and entertainment complex called **Gloria** in Eagle Beach for first-run movies, a children's play park, and lots of dining options like P.F. Chang's.

You can also enjoy some first-rate pampering at one of the island's many premium spas—maybe an aloe-based treatment to soothe your overly sunned skin? Or how about a couple's massage by the sea under a tiki hut? If you want more action, the casinos are always ready to receive you. Some are open 24 hours a day, and sometimes they offer daytime bingo.

Best Tours

Tours

You can see the main sights in one day, but set aside two days to really meander. Guided tours are your best option if you have only a short time.

TOUR OPERATORS

There are many first-rate tour operators on Aruba, and the adventures range from wild and crazy jeep safaris in the outback to Segway tours along the coast to sea and sand discovery and even historical, art, and foodie walking tours. A good way to get your bearings is to take a bus tour around the island's main highlights—it's a small island so it will not take more than half a day—with a well-established company like De Palm Tours.

Aruba Walking Tours

Explore the heartbeat of One Happy Island and learn all about its fascinating history on the Aruba Historic Cultural Downtown Walking Tour, which lasts about 2½ hours and covers about 30 stops including a cooking demonstration. They also offer a foodie adventure at night called Fusions of World Food Tour that stops at five places that have intrinsic ties. Complimentary pickup is included from most hotels (but not drop-off), and private and custom tours are also available. ■TIP→ **The big metal solar tree sculpture at the meeting spot has smartphone charging outlets within it.** ⊠ *Zoutmanstraat 1, Oranjestad* ☎ *297/699–0995* ⊕ *www.arubawalkingtours.com* 🎫 *From $39* 🕐 *No tours Sun.*

BIKE TOURS

Guided bike tours are offered with Green Bike and Aruba BikeTours. Rancho Notorious offers mountain biking tours. Aruba Motorcycle Tours is a unique way to see the island.

Aruba E-Bike Tours

This operator offers fat-tire electric bicycles that can give you a power boost when you need it. Visitors can choose any one of four hour-long guided tours around the island. There are daily departures in the early morning and at sunset, and points of interest include the California Lighthouse and Alto Vista Chapel. Helmets and visibility vests are included. Children must be 12 and over. ⊠ *Paseo Herencia Mall, J. E. Irausquin Blvd. 328A, Palm Beach* ☎ *297/592–5550* ⊕ *www.arubaebiketours.com* 🎫 *From $45.*

Aruba Motorcycle Tours

Hog fans will adore this novel way to tour Aruba. On your own Harley with a rental, or in one of their guided group tours—a four-hour trip that takes only the back roads to bring you the island's best sites—you will enjoy the open

road like a rebel with this outfit. A motorcycle license and $1,000 deposit is required with each tour. For rentals alone, a $2,000 deposit is required. Helmets are supplied, and pickup and drop-off at hotels is offered. All renters and group riders must be over 21. ⊠ *Jaburibari 16-C, Noord* ☎ *297/641–7818* ⊕ *www. arubamotorcycletours.com* ☞ *Tours from $50 (on top of rental).*

Green Bike Aruba Tours
The same company that supplies the grab-and-go shared bike kiosks around the island also offers two group-bike tours. One explores the beaches around the California Lighthouse and includes a stop there, and the other explores downtown and the Linear Park. Both tours include a well-informed guide, a bike cooler basket with snacks and water, and free Wi-Fi as you tour. Bring or wear your bathing suit as they take swim stops, too. ⊠ *Ponto 69, Oranjestad* ☎ *297/594–6368* ⊕ *www. greenbikearuba.com* ☞ *From $39.*

Rancho Notorious
If mountain biking is more your thing, tours are offered through the Aruban countryside on old donkey trails—there are more than 200 mountain bike trails on the island—for half or full

days. Bikes are TREK aluminum mountain bikes. ⊠ *Boronca-na, Noord* ☎ *297/586–0508* ⊕ *www.ranchonotorious.com.*

BOAT TOURS
Snorkeling and sunset party cruises are the norm, but some also include dinner or have dinner on shore after your voyage. Most seaborne tours depart from Palm Beach at either Pelican Pier, De Palm Pier, or the Hadicurari Pier, with a few exceptions departing from downtown Oranjestad. There are also semi-submarine and submarine tours with Atlantis Submarines (operated by De Palm Tours), which operates a 65-foot air-conditioned sub that takes 48 passengers 95 to 130 feet below the surface along Barcadera Reef. The two-hour trip (including boat transfer to the submarine platform and 50-minute plunge) has garnered multiple awards for best tour and one for green operations. Make reservations one day in advance. Another option is the *Seaworld Explorer,* a semisubmersible also operated by Atlantis Submarines that allows you to view Aruba's marine habitat from 6 feet below the surface.

CONTACTS De Palm Tours.
⊠ *L. G. Smith Blvd. 142, Oranjestad* ☎ *297/582–4400, 800/766–6016* ⊕ *www.depalm. com.* **Pelican Adventures.** ⊠ *J. E.*

Best Tours

Irausquin Blvd. 232, Oranjestad
☏ *297/587–2302* ⊕ *www.*
pelican-aruba.com.

FOOD TOURS

Fusion of the World Food Tour

Discover five different dining
spots for tapas and drinks—
each with an inherent connec-
tion to Aruba—and all within
walking distance of each other
in downtown Oranjestad. This
two-and-a-half-hour foodie tour
takes place in the evening with
a local guide who will also fill
you in on some history and
highlights of the downtown
attractions and neighborhoods
you are exploring. The pace is
leisurely and complimentary
pickup and drop-off from the
major resort areas can be
included. ✉ *Cosecha building,*
Zoutmanstraat 1 ✛ *Across*
the street from the big yellow
Cosecha building, look for the
Aruba Walking Tours meeting
point sign ☏ *297/699–0995*
⊕ *www.arubawalkingtours.*
com/aruba-food-tour 🎟 *$79.*

Kukoo Kunuku Party & Foodie Tours

Best known for their wild and
crazy barhopping tours aboard
brightly painted red party
buses, this outfit also dials it
down a notch for their foodie
tours like the Dinner & Nightlife
Tour that includes a sunset
champagne toast or the Wine
On Down The Road tour, which
features an onboard sommelier
and stops at some of Aruba's
finest dining spots for wine
and tapas. They also offer a
Happy Hour tour. ✉ *Oranjestad*
☏ *297/586–2010* ⊕ *www.*
kukookunuku.com 🎟 *From*
$50.

SPECIALTY TOURS

Aruba's interior is rugged and
rocky and best explored with
an all-terrain vehicle, especially
if you want to explore the cacti-studded countryside or visit
the natural pool or other incredible landmarks like the small
natural bridges or the wild
coast. The island's largest tour
operators like De Palm Tours
and ABC Tours offer the most
choices when it comes to jeep
safaris and UTV tours, but if
you want to go it alone, then
it's best to rent a rough-and-
tumble vehicle from a company
that specializes in them like Off
Road Evolution Aruba.

ABC Tours

Jeep and UTV tour itineraries
include visits to Aruba's interesting historical sites as well
as natural attractions. Private
curated tours also available
including Sea Scooters and
GoPros. ✉ *Schotlandstraat 61,*
Oranjestad ☏ *297/582-5600*
⊕ *abc-aruba.com* 🎟 *Starting*
at $150.

On the Calender

YEAR-ROUND
Bon Bini Festival. Local music and dance festival Tuesday nights at Fort Zoutman. ⊕ *aruba-regatta.com*

Island Festival. Monthly cultural music, dance, and food event in San Nicolas. ⊕ *www.island-festivalaruba.com*

Meet San Nicolas. Monthly cultural street party.

JANUARY–MARCH
Carnival. Weeks of parties and cultural events precede this two-day street party in late February or early March. ⊕ *aruba-regatta.com*

FEBRUARY
Carnival Grand Parade. The culmination of Carnival celebrations in downtown Oranjestad.

MARCH
National Flag and Anthem Day. March 18th brings celebrations to the streets. ⊕ *aruba-regatta. com*

APRIL
King's Day. On April 27, Aruba celebrates Dutch King Willem's birthday with outdoor activities.

Eat Local's Food Truck Festival. Last week of April in downtown Oranjestad. ⊕ *aruba-regatta.com*

MAY
Soul Beach Music Festival. Memorial Day Weekend event attracts famous international music talents. ⊕ *www.soulbeach.net*

JUNE
KLM Aruba Marathon. Marathon day also includes a half marathon, a 10K, and a 5K. ⊕ *arubainternationalmarathon. com*

JULY
Aruba Hi-Winds. An annual massive windsurfing and kiteboarding competition with parties. ⊕ *hiwindsaruba.com*

AUGUST
Aruba I Do. On August 22, hundreds of couples renew vows on Eagle Beach. ⊕ *aruba-regatta.com*

Aruba International Regatta. Three days of great boat races and parties in mid-August. ⊕ *aruba-regatta.com*

SEPTEMBER
Aruba Reef Care Project Clean-Up. Island-wide local and visitor event attracting hundreds, great after-parties. ⊕ *caribbeanseajazz.com*

Casabari Jazz Festival Jazz festival located at the base of the Casibari rock formations. ⊕ *casibarifestival.com*

On the Calender

OCTOBER

Eat Local Restaurant Month. The month of October offers local dining specials and events. ⊕ *aruba-regatta.com*

Island TakeOver Festival. 4-day music festival with local and international artists. ⊕ *islandtakeover.com*

NOVEMBER

Aruba Art Fair. San Nicolas invites international artists to permanently beautify sunrise city. ⊕ *www.arubaartfair.com*

Aruba Fashion Week. Annual event with fashion shows, trunk shows, and more.

Aruba Open Beach Tennis Championships. A massive international tennis competition the second week of November with parties. ⊕ *www.arubabeachtennisopen. com*

DECEMBER

Dande Festival. Local musicians welcome the new year with original songs and competitions. ⊕ *www.aruba.com*

Winter Wonderland Christmas Market. Located at Renaissance Marketplace, the event features live music, food, an ice skating court, and kids' activities. ⊕ *www.visitaruba. com*

ORANJESTAD

Updated by
Susan Campbell

◉ Sights	🍴 Restaurants	🛏 Hotels	🛍 Shopping	🍸 Nightlife
★★★☆☆	★★★★☆	★★☆☆☆	★★★★☆	★★★★☆

NEIGHBORHOOD SNAPSHOT

TOP EXPERIENCES

- **Luxury Shopping:** Downtown's upscale shops have jewelry, watches, and brand-name fashions.
- **Try Your Luck:** Visit glitzy world-class casinos where you can seduce lady luck.
- **Walking Tours:** Explore downtown's culture, history, and food with Aruba Walking Tours.
- **Trolley Tour:** Take the free trolley to preview the eclectic maze of superb shopping and dining options.
- **Surfside Beach:** Grab a green bike and head out on the paved seaside trail to discover this lovely little urban beach.

GETTING HERE AND AROUND

About 15 minutes from the airport, Oranjestad is accessible by car, taxi, or public bus. The bus stops at most major resorts as well as the downtown terminal and all the best attractions. There's a pedestrian-only walkway and a free Downtown Trolley.

PLANNING YOUR TIME

Downtown can be crowded when the cruise ships are in port; check the port authority website to see the schedule if you want to avoid the crunch. Sundays are sleepier as many of the smaller shops close, but the main malls remain open late. Traffic can be intense at rush hours, and parking can be tricky at peak business hours (there are free lots including the one behind the Renaissance Marketplace), but never park between yellow lines or you'll get a boot. Downtown is safe, but stick to the main streets at night.

VIEWFINDER

- The original giant "I Love Aruba" sign has been moved from the marina area in front of the parliament buildings to the cruise ship welcome area across from the local market. And there is another colorful oversized Aruba sign in Plaza Tourismo on Surfside Beach. But why go cliché when you can snap a selfie with some cool neon blue ceramic horses (www.paardenbaai.com)? You'll find them popping up in surprising places all around the downtown grid. But please don't mount them; they are fragile ceramic art meant to be admired, not ridden!

Aruba's historic port capital city Oranjestad has always had a colorful Dutch colonial charm, but the past few years have seen a major face-lift and renewal throughout Downtown to better accommodate a growing local population and better welcome the 2 million-plus visitors it sees each year.

Aruba's capital is easily explored on foot. Its palm-lined central thoroughfare runs between old and new pastel-painted buildings of typical Dutch design (Spanish influence is also evident in some of the architecture), and guided walking tours help you discover its history, culture, and food. There are a lot of malls with boutiques and shops—the Renaissance Mall carries high-end luxury items and designer fashions. Massive renovations continue to give Main Street (aka Caya G. F. Betico Croes), behind the Renaissance Marina Resort, a whole new lease on life with boutique malls, shops, and restaurants opening next to well-loved family-run businesses.

The pedestrian-only walkway and resting areas have unclogged the streets, and the free ecotrolley is a great way to get around if you don't want to walk—you can hop on and hop off as you like. Across from the cruise terminal, you'll find a huge market with locally made wares; directly behind it is the new Bochincha Entertainment venue, a massive two-story alfresco emporium made from old shipping containers that are chock-full of modern food truck–style options with music at night. The Linear Park (an ongoing project that will connect Downtown to the main tourist beaches by sidewalks and boardwalks) begins in Oranjestad and runs all the way to the airport, providing locals and visitors alike with a scenic paved path along the sea to walk, bike, or jog. It's also peppered with free public fitness equipment.

The urban Surfside Beach is where you'll find upscale seaside lounging, funky beach bars, and a massive floating water park full of fun for the family, just minutes from the downtown core. It's also an ideal spot for plane-spotting as they arrive right overhead.

Sights

Aruba Aloe Museum & Factory

FACTORY | Aruba has the ideal conditions to grow the aloe vera plant. It's an important export, and there are aloe stores all over the island. The museum and factory tour reveal the process of extracting the serum to make many products used for beauty, health, and healing. Guided or self-guided tours are available in English, Dutch, Spanish, and Papiamento. There's a store to purchase their products on-site, and they are also available online. ■**TIP→ Look for their reef-safe sunscreen; it's available island-wide.** ⊠ *Pitastraat 115, Oranjestad* ☎ *800/952–7822* ⊕ *www.arubaaloe. com* ⌨ *Free.*

★ Aruba Linear Park

CITY PARK | FAMILY | Plaza Turismo, off Surfside Beach, is the anchor of the Linear Park which, when completed, will connect both main tourist beaches along the coast by boardwalks and walking paths. The first leg—a smooth paved biking and jogging trail that runs from downtown Oranjestad along the sea all the way to the airport—is complete. There are many cafés, bars, and snack stops along the way, and there are also fitness pit stops with free-to-use public fitness equipment. It's a popular stretch for local fun runs and fitness initiatives, and locals and visitors use the easy-to-access Green Bike rental kiosks. Much like "Bixi Bike" operations, you can use your credit card to grab a bike and then leave it at another stop. The plaza has also become a go-to spot for cultural events and outdoor entertainment. A new portion was added in 2021 to the Malmok area that ends at Fisherman's Huts Beach. When complete, the Linear Park will be the longest of its kind in the entire Caribbean. ⊠ *Surfside Beach and Malmok,* ⌨ *Free.*

★ Cosecha Aruba Oranjestad

STORE/MALL | One of the many historic buildings repurposed as an attraction over the past few years, this arts foundation displays only the works of local artisans. The building houses workshops, a gallery, and a design shop where visitors can purchase exquisite souvenirs. All artisans selling and showing wares here must be "Seyo" certified, a national seal that ensures that all work is locally made, of excellent quality, and reflects Aruban heritage. The beautifully restored 100-year-old mansion in which it's located is worth a visit on its own. Check their website for many special events like "Art, Sangria & Tapas Wednesdays." There's another Cosecha in San Nicolas with art workshops for visitors. ⊠ *Zoutmanstraat 1, Oranjestad* ☎ *297/578–8709* ⊕ *www.arubacosecha.com* ⌨ *Free* ☉ *Closed Mon. and Tues.*

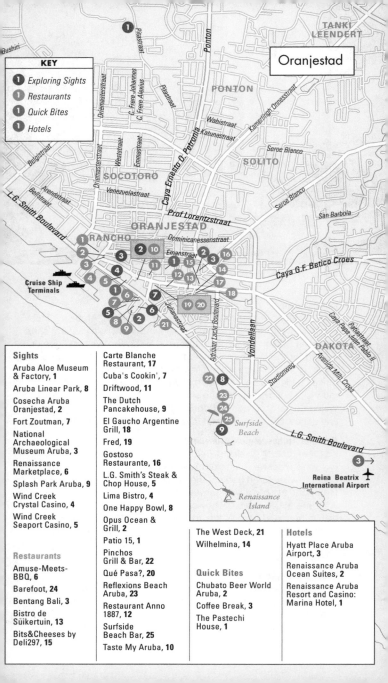

KEY

- **1** Exploring Sights
- **1** Restaurants
- **1** Quick Bites
- **1** Hotels

Oranjestad

Cruise Ship Terminals

Sights

Aruba Aloe Museum & Factory, **1**

Aruba Linear Park, **8**

Cosecha Aruba Oranjestad, **2**

Fort Zoutman, **7**

National Archaeological Museum Aruba, **3**

Renaissance Marketplace, **6**

Splash Park Aruba, **9**

Wind Creek Crystal Casino, **4**

Wind Creek Seaport Casino, **5**

Restaurants

Amuse-Meets-BBQ, **6**

Barefoot, **24**

Bentang Bali, **3**

Bistro de Suikertuin, **13**

Bits&Cheeses by Deli297, **15**

Carte Blanche Restaurant, **17**

Cuba's Cookin', **7**

Driftwood, **11**

The Dutch Pancakehouse, **9**

El Gaucho Argentine Grill, **18**

Fred, **19**

Gostoso Restaurante, **16**

L.G. Smith's Steak & Chop House, **5**

Lima Bistro, **4**

One Happy Bowl, **8**

Opus Ocean & Grill, **2**

Patio 15, **1**

Pinchos Grill & Bar, **22**

Qué Pasa?, **20**

Reflexions Beach Aruba, **23**

Restaurant Anno 1887, **12**

Surfside Beach Bar, **25**

Taste My Aruba, **10**

The West Deck, **21**

Wilhelmina, **14**

Quick Bites

Chubato Beer World Aruba, **2**

Coffee Break, **3**

The Pastechi House, **1**

Hotels

Hyatt Place Aruba Airport, **3**

Renaissance Aruba Ocean Suites, **2**

Renaissance Aruba Resort and Casino: Marina Hotel, **1**

Built in 1798 by the Dutch army, Fort Zoutman is Aruba's oldest structure.

Fort Zoutman

MILITARY SIGHT | One of the island's oldest edifices, Aruba's historic fort was built in 1796 and played an important role in skirmishes between British and Curaçao troops in 1803. The Willem III Tower, named for the Dutch monarch of that time, was added in 1868 to serve as a lighthouse. Over time the fort has been a government office building, a police station, a prison, and a small museum (now closed). This is also the site of the weekly Tuesday-night welcome party called the Bon Bini festival, with local music, food, and dance. ⌧ *Zoutmanstraat, Oranjestad* ☎ *297/588–5199*.

National Archaeological Museum Aruba

HISTORY MUSEUM | Walking around downtown Oranjestad, you can't miss this massive mustard yellow and olive-green complex. This beautifully restored heritage home was once owned by the Ecury family and it's been transformed into an ultra-modern museum with interactive exhibits showcasing over 5,000 years of Amerindian culture and Aruba's ties to it. More than 10,000 artifacts are on display, and special exhibits by local artists are also hosted on a regular basis. ⌧ *Schelpstraat 42, Oranjestad* ⊕ *namaruba.org* ⌧ *Free* ☉ *Closed weekends.*

Renaissance Marketplace

STORE/MALL | **FAMILY** | The complex beside the Oranjestad marina and the park around it is the place where you're most likely to happen upon some great free entertainment, including pop-up festivals. Although there's live entertainment every night at the far end in the common area bandstand, most of the bars and

cafés also invite their own bands. You'll also find a casino, movie theaters, and arty little shops that are open late. Occasionally, there's a big gala music festival, and every Friday night there's a local artisans market from 7–10 pm. Even if there's no planned additional activity, it's a wonderful spot to explore in the evening to experience a truly enchanting tropical night full of colorful lights and sounds along the water. ⊠ *Marina, L.G. Smith Blvd. 82, Oranjestad* ☎ *297/583–6000* ⊕ *www.shoprenaissancearuba.com* ☞ *Free.*

Splash Park Aruba

WATER PARK | FAMILY | Few people realize that you can swim in downtown Oranjestad at Surfside Beach just off the new Linear Park. And families can enjoy a unique attraction there as well. Splash Park Aruba is a huge inflatable maze of obstacles, jungle gyms, swings, slides, and climbing towers. It's a great way to cool off after Downtown shopping and sightseeing with lots of aqua fun for the whole family (children six and over only). ⊠ *Surfside Beach, Oranjestad* ☎ *297/594–1002* ⊕ *www.splashparkaruba.com* ☞ *$18 (admission for 1 hr. only)* ⊗ *Closed weekdays.* ⚲ *None required.*

CASINOS

Wind Creek Crystal Casino

CASINO | Adorned with Austrian crystal chandeliers and gold-leaf columns, the Renaissance Aruba's glittering casino evokes Monaco's grand establishments. The Salon Privé offers serious gamblers a private room for baccarat, roulette, and high-stakes blackjack. This casino is popular among cruise-ship passengers, who stroll over from the port to watch and play in slot tournaments and bet on sporting events. Luxury car giveaways are also a big draw there. It's open 24 hours and there's live entertainment Tuesday through Sunday. ⊠ *Renaissance Aruba Resort & Casino, L. G. Smith Blvd. 82, Oranjestad* ☎ *297/583–6000* ⊕ *www.windcreekaruba.com.*

★ Wind Creek Seaport Casino

CASINO | A super-lively and fun casino right on the waterfront and across the street from the lively Renaissance Marketplace, this place has more than 300 modern slots as well as four blackjack tables, Caribbean stud, roulette, regular poker, Texas Hold'em, and daily bingo starting at noon. They also have state-of-the-art race and sports book operations. Open until 4 am. ⊠ *L. G. Smith Blvd. 9, Oranjestad* ☎ *297/583–6000 ext. 6318* ⊕ *www.windcreekaruba.com.*

Beaches

Renaissance Island

BEACH | FAMILY | This tiny tropical oasis is accessible only to guests of the Renaissance Marina and Renaissance Ocean Suite hotels unless you buy an expensive day pass, which is not always available. Free boat shuttles pick up guests in the lower lobby or from the marina. Iguana Beach is family-friendly, while Flamingo Beach is limited to adults and hosts half a dozen resident flamingos. (Children may visit the flamingos for a photo op daily from 10 to 11 am but must have an adult present.) The waters are clear and full of colorful fish; swimming is in a protected area, and there's a full-service restaurant, a beach bar, and waiter service on the beach. Rent a cabana for more luxuries. If you book a spa treatment, you can spend the rest of the day on the island for free. **Amenities:** food and drink; toilets; showers. **Best for:** swimming; water sports; snorkeling. ⊠ *Oranjestad* ⊹ *Accessible by water taxi only from the Renaissance Aruba Hotel & Marina* ☎ *297/583–6000* ⊕ *www.marriott.com* 🎫 *Day pass $125.*

Surfside Beach

BEACH | FAMILY | Accessible by public bus, car, or taxi, this little beach has come back to life just outside downtown Oranjestad with beach bars, access to the paved Linear Park, and Plaza Turismo. It's also the location of Splash Park Aruba, an inflatable water park. This is an ideal spot to stop for a dip when cycling or jogging along the bike path or strolling around the town. **Amenities:** food and drink; parking (free); toilets; water sports. **Best for:** swimming; partiers; sunsets. ⊠ *L. G. Smith Blvd., Oranjestad* ⊹ *Just before airport compound* ⊕ *www.aruba.com/us/explore/surfside-beach.*

 Restaurants

Amuse-Meets-BBQ

$$$ | SOUTHERN | FAMILY | Chef Patrick van der Donk, well-known for his French-inspired (now shuttered) Amuse Bistro and Amuse Sunset restaurants, has turned his considerable culinary skills to BBQ. Specialties are beyond your basic smoked fare like tender pulled pork quesadillas, but if you really want to chow down Southern-style, don't miss their all-you-can-eat ribs night on Saturdays or their Family Platter Fridays that features a full assortment of their cuisine. **Known for:** home-made chorizo sausages; Southern-style BBQ ribs; Angus Prime beef brisket. Ⓢ *Average main: $25* ⊠ *Renaissance Marketplace, L.G. Smith Blvd. 9, Oranjestad* ☎ *297/586–7008* ⊕ *www.facebook.com/AmuseAruba.*

★ Barefoot

$$$$ | **CONTEMPORARY** | One of Aruba's most popular toes-in-the-sand spots (even their indoor dining has sand on the floor), it's all about creative, international fusion cuisine, comprehensive upscale wine choices, and superb signature cocktails in an ultimate barefoot-luxury setting. The sunset views are always spectacular. **Known for:** great service and consistent quality fare; romantic toes-in-the-sand dining; creative fusions like lobster cappuccino bisque. $ *Average main: $35* ⊠ *L. G. Smith Blvd. 1, Oranjestad* ⚓ *on Surfside Beach* ☎ *297/588–9824* ⊕ *www.bare-footaruba.com* ☾ *No lunch.*

Bentang Bali

$$ | **INDONESIAN** | The Dutch still have strong culinary ties to Indonesia, so this welcome newcomer to Downtown offers an ideal place to indulge in quality comfort food from that corner of the globe. Exotic and traditional Asian specialties also abound, and this is one of the few places on the island where you can sample the elusive "rijsttafel" (rice table), a large assortment of small dishes meant to be shared by a group. **Known for:** an eclectic selection of seafood like king crab and calamari; homemade black pasta and dumplings; large selection of vegetarian dishes. $ *Average main: $15* ⊠ *Havenstraat 36 B, Oranjestad* ☎ *297/280–0440* ⊕ *www.facebook.com/bentangbali* ☾ *Closed Mon.*

★ Bistro De Suikertuin

$$ | **INTERNATIONAL** | This charming bistro dining spot is the quintessential meeting place for locals and visitors alike seeking great signature cocktails, creative tapas, quality coffee, and healthy lunch options, as well as a full dinner menu with dishes that range from chicken cordon bleu to beef tenderloin with Dutch potatoes. Suikertuin means "sugar garden" in Dutch and this spot is so named for the yellow sugar birds that frequent the courtyard behind this historic colonial heritage house. **Known for:** lovely shaded courtyard with big tables for group socializing; elegant royal high tea and high wine services; Aruban and Indonesian dishes like keshi yena and nasi goreng. $ *Average main: $20* ⊠ *Wilhelmi-nastraat 64, Oranjestad* ☎ *297/582–6322* ⊕ *www.desuikertuin. com* ☾ *Closed Sun.*

★ Bits&Cheeses by Deli297

$$ | **INTERNATIONAL** | What began as a catering company became so popular that they decided to open a brick-and-mortar café in the heart of downtown Oranjestad, so now you can dine inside their cheery new space to enjoy breakfast or lunch and an amazing selection of gourmet cheeses, quality charcuterie, and a surprising selection of fine wines, too. Grab one of their BC boxes to

go for a perfect picnic, or a lavish platter of goodies to entertain guests back at your hotel. **Known for:** creative paninis and pastas; quality catering and delivery of gourmet fare; special baskets and boards of meats and cheeses. $ *Average main: $20* ✉ *Wilhelminastraat 63, Oranjestad* ☎ *297/566–5264* ⊕ *www.facebook.com/bitsandcheeses* ⊗ *Closed Sun. and Mon.*

Carte Blanche Restaurant

$$$$ | **ECLECTIC** | Next door to a sister restaurant of Wilhelmina, this intimate chef's table experience for 14 people is set in a tropical garden. Created by Chef Dennis van Daatselaar, being open-minded to new taste experiences is the focus here, so expect the unexpected, and though every dish might not be to your individual taste, the overall adventure is typically well applauded by local and visiting foodies. **Known for:** an enjoyable culinary adventure; consistently creative quality cuisine; an impressive wine list. $ *Average main: $109* ✉ *Wilhelminastraat 74, Oranjestad* ☎ *297/586–3339* ⊕ *www.carteblanchearuba.com* ⊗ *Closed Mon. No lunch.*

★ Cuba's Cookin'

$$$ | **CUBAN** | This red-hot landmark establishment in the heart of Renaissance Marketplace specializes in traditional Havana specialties and is the only spot on Aruba where you can enjoy an authentic Cuban sandwich for lunch. Their boast of having the best mojitos in town is a fair claim, and there's even a surprisingly good selection of gluten-free, vegetarian, and vegan fare on offer. **Known for:** an impressive selection of original Cuban art; melt-in-your-mouth ropa vieja (Cuba's national skirt steak dish); hot live music and alfresco dancing seven nights a week. $ *Average main: $28* ✉ *Renaissance Marketplace, L. G. Smith Blvd. 82, Oranjestad* ☎ *297/588–0627* ⊕ *www.cubascookin.com.*

Driftwood

$$$ | **CARIBBEAN** | **FAMILY** | Opened in 1986, this rustic, nautical-themed restaurant is owned and operated by the Merryweather family. It's justifiably famous for serving up the freshest catch of the day caught by the owners themselves. **Known for:** friendly service and warm atmosphere; family-recipe, hearty fish soup; boat-to-table fresh fish and other seafood. $ *Average main: $30* ✉ *Klipstraat 12, Oranjestad* ☎ *297/583–2515* ⊕ *www.driftwoodaruba.com* ⊗ *Closed Sun.*

★ The Dutch Pancakehouse

$$ | **DUTCH** | **FAMILY** | Dutch pancakes are unlike North American-style flapjacks since they can be both savory and sweet, offering opportunities for breakfast, lunch, and dinner, and this legendary spot in the Renaissance Marketplace is considered the absolute best place to try them. More like thin crepes, they can

Most Aruba restaurants are casual and fun places for a drink and a meal.

be covered in (or stuffed with) a multitude of ingredients, which might include meats, vegetables, and cheeses. **Known for:** consistently good-quality fare and friendly service; over 50 styles of sweet and savory Dutch-style pancakes; a surprising selection of excellent schnitzels. ⑤ *Average main: $15* ⊠ *Renaissance Marketplace, L. G. Smith Blvd. 9, Oranjestad* ☎ *297/583–7180* ⊕ *www. thedutchpancakehouse.com.*

El Gaucho Argentine Grill
$$$$ | **STEAKHOUSE** | **FAMILY** | Aruba's original go-to mecca for carnivores since 1977, El Gaucho is famous for meat served in mammoth portions. Though to be honest, it's not all about meat; seafood platters are something to consider as well. **Known for:** strolling musicians who create a fun and boisterous atmosphere; 16-ounce Gaucho steak; largest shish kebab on the island. ⑤ *Average main: $40* ⊠ *Wilhelminastraat 80, Oranjestad* ☎ *297/582–3677* ⊕ *www.elgaucho-aruba.com* ☾ *Closed Mon.*

Fred
$$$$ | **INTERNATIONAL** | Chef Fred Wanders offers a chef's table experience in downtown Oranjestad with a five-course surprise menu in an intimate venue that seems more like his home kitchen than a dining spot. Optional wine pairings cost extra but are available by the glass and can be added to any course (or all courses). **Known for:** reservations required and adults-only; an intimate and excellent dining experience; creative international cuisine. ⑤ *Average main: $110* ⊠ *Wilhelminastraat 18, Oranjestad* ⊹ *Upstairs*

from Qué Pasa? restaurant ☎ *297/565–2324* ⊕ *www.fredaruba. com* ⊗ *Closed weekends.*

Gostoso Restaurante

$$$ | **CARIBBEAN** | **FAMILY** | Locals adore the magical mixture of Portuguese, Aruban, and international dishes on offer at this consistently excellent establishment. The decor walks a fine line between kitschy and cozy, but the atmosphere is relaxed and informal and outdoor seating is available. **Known for:** popular local hangout; hearty Venezuelan-style mixed grill; large choice of authentic Aruba stobas (stews). ⑤ *Average main: $28* ⊠ *Caya Ing. Roland H. Lacle 12, Oranjestad* ☎ *297/588–0053* ⊕ *www.facebook.com/ Gostosoaruba* ⊗ *Closed Mon.*

L. G. Smith's Steak & Chop House

$$$$ | **STEAKHOUSE** | A study in teak, cream, and black, this fine steak house offers some of the best beef on the island. Subdued lighting and cascading water create an elegant atmosphere, and the view over the harbor makes for an exceptional dining experience. **Known for:** excellent wine list and stellar signature cocktails; 4-course beef and wine tasting menu from around the world; USDA-certified Angus beef. ⑤ *Average main: $50* ⊠ *Renaissance Aruba Marina Resort & Casino, L. G. Smith Blvd. 82, Oranjestad* ☎ *297/523–6195* ⊕ *www.lgsmiths.com.*

Lima Bistro

$$$ | **PERUVIAN** | Considering its secret location in the bottom corner of Harbour House, this adorable little Peruvian-themed escape has already garnered a big buzz for its food likely because owner Chef Teddy Bouroncle is well-known for his culinary talents from his tenure at the Aruba Marriott. Dine inside or out and enjoy traditional Peruvian dishes like Lomo Saltado or their special take on ceviche. **Known for:** warm and inviting family-run atmosphere; creative takes on traditional Peruvian fare; elevated street food and killer authentic cocktails. ⑤ *Average main: $25* ⊠ *Harbour House, Weststraat 2, Oranjestad* ☎ *297/281–3810* ⊕ *www.facebook.com/ limabistroaruba* ⊗ *Closed Sun. No lunch.*

★ One Happy Bowl

$$ | **VEGETARIAN** | You need not be a vegan or seeking gluten-free options to thoroughly enjoy the creative takes on the strictly plant-based fare at this happy little nook, but if you are, it's bound to be your new paradise. It's tiny though, so if you intend to dine in, reservations are a must, though there is a bustling take-out and delivery business, too. **Known for:** vegan high tea first Sunday of every month; create your own plant-based poke bowls; all-day plant-based breakfast specials. ⑤ *Average main: $13.50* ⊠ *Renaissance*

Marketplace, L. G. Smith Blvd. 9, Oranjestad ☎ *297/641–8919 Whats App* ⊕ *onehappybowl.com* ☾ *No dinner.*

Opus Ocean & Grill

$$$ | INTERNATIONAL | Mauve mood lighting and enchanting fairy lights set the stage for this intimate little family-run restaurant specializing in seafood and grilled meats. The menu is not comprehensive, but what they do very well includes beautifully prepared shrimp and grilled-to-perfection tomahawk steaks; choosing Surf & Turf of course is a no-brainer to enjoy the best of both worlds. **Known for:** rotating chef's specials like paella and seafood pasta; excellent homemade fish soup; attentive and knowledgeable service. ⑤ *Average main: $25* ⊠ *Havenstraat 36 B, Oranjestad* ☎ *297/280–0120* ⊕ *www.facebook.com/OPUSARUBA* ☾ *No dinner Sun.*

★ Patio 15

$$ | INTERNATIONAL | A very exciting new addition to Downtown's backstreets, Patio 15 is set in a stunningly restored two-story heritage house with a humongous patio and outdoor event space. The food, drink, and entertainment venue has become an instant hit with both locals and visitors alike who enjoy creative craft cocktails along with intriguing tapas-sized mains like watermelon feta pizza or fried spam sliders with plantains and Madam Jeanette's hot sauce. **Known for:** neon light shows and exciting special events; weekend gathering spot with live or DJ music and large dance space; trendy tapas and oversized signature sangria by the glass. ⑤ *Average main: $12* ⊠ *Weststraat 15, Oranjestad* ☎ *297/588–1515* ⊕ *www.patio15aruba.com* ☾ *Closed Mon. No lunch.*

★ Pinchos Grill & Bar

$$$$ | ECLECTIC | One of the most romantic settings on the island is highlighted by enchanting twinkling lights strung over the water on a pier. *Pinchos* ("skewers" in Spanish) offers a fairly extensive menu of both meat and seafood skewers in addition to more creative main courses. Boursin-and-apple-stuffed pork tenderloin and maple BBQ bourbon cowboy pinchos keep carnivores sated, and there's vegan couscous, too. **Known for:** excellent personalized service; romantic pier-side atmosphere; signature sangria. ⑤ *Average main: $35* ⊠ *L. G. Smith Blvd. 7, Oranjestad* ☎ *297/583–2666* ⊕ *www.pinchosaruba.com* ☾ *No lunch.*

Qué Pasa?

$$$ | ECLECTIC | This funky eatery is also part art gallery, and despite the name, the fare here is not Mexican but much more international with some real surprises like a comprehensive sushi menu. The staff is helpful and friendly, and creative chef specials change

often. **Known for:** all-you-can-eat sushi Wednesdays and weekend brunch; special wine-and-food pairing nights; an eclectic assortment of international dishes. ⑤ *Average main: $30* ⊠ *Wilhelminastraat 18, Oranjestad* ☎ *297/583–4888* ⊕ *www.quepasaaruba.com* ☉ *No lunch Mon.–Thurs.*

Reflexions Beach Aruba

$$$ | INTERNATIONAL | A sophisticated upscale spot on the water minutes from downtown Oranjestad does its best to replicate the South Beach Miami scene with luxe cabanas and daybeds, and beach and pool service around a chic seaside bar. It can be lively at nights when there are musical events, but dinner is mostly laid-back in high style with a good selection of quality cuts of meats and fresh fish and seafood, plus a good selection of fine champagnes. **Known for:** stunning sunsets and chic vibe; superb creative tapas and signature cocktails; great pool right on the beach. ⑤ *Average main: $25* ⊠ *L. G. Smith Blvd. 1A, Surfside Beach, Oranjestad* ☎ *297/582–0153* ⊕ *www.reflexionsaruba.com.*

Restaurant Anno 1887

$$$ | FRENCH | Those still mourning the loss of two of Aruba's most beloved dining spots—Chez Mathilde and Le Dome—can dry their eyes, because some of the original players of those establishments have teamed up to create the same type of classic French experience in downtown Oranjestad. Expect impeccable personal service and iconic French fare like *tournedos au poivre* (beef in red wine) and coq au vin but vegan options can also be requested on-site. **Known for:** prix-fixe five-course chef tasting menu; Classic French dishes like bouillabaisse de Marseille and chocolate or Grand Marnier soufflé; quality ingredients always prepared "a la minute". ⑤ *Average main: $30* ⊠ *Wilheminastraat 27, Oranjestad* ☎ *297/583–0020* ⊕ *www.restaurantanno1877.com* ☉ *No lunch. Closed Sun.*

Surfside Beach Bar

$$ | INTERNATIONAL | FAMILY | Enjoy cool and creative cocktails and beach shack eats in the afternoon on a pristine stretch of white sand on an aqua sea just minutes from downtown Oranjestad. The fun and friendly vibe includes beach service, lounge and umbrella rentals, and happy hour drink specials. **Known for:** hearty Dutch-style breakfasts Friday–Sunday; Sunday barbecue noon–7 pm; casual fare like burgers, spicy shrimp, fish-and-chips, and create-your-own pizzas. ⑤ *Average main: $12* ⊠ *Surfside Beach, Oranjestad* ☎ *297/280–6584* ⊕ *www.surfsidearuba.com.*

★ Taste My Aruba

$$$$ | CARIBBEAN | What began as a teeny-tiny café tucked under the historic Cosecha Arts building has grown to become downtown's hottest spot for fresh fish and locally caught lobster

dinners thanks to the personality and culinary skills of owners Nathaly de Mey and her talented nephew Chef Derwin Tromp. Dedicated to serving locally sourced fare as much as possible, the menu changes daily depending on the bounty, but rarely disappoints. **Known for:** outstanding personal service and welcoming atmosphere; expertly prepared giant local lobster and fresh fish straight from the boat; authentic local experience and locally sourced fare. ⑤ *Average main: $32* ⊠ *Cosecha Building, Zoutman Straat 1, Oranjestad* ⚓ *Tucked beneath the Cosecha building* ☎ *297/588–1600* ⊕ *www.tastemyaruba.com* ☾ *Closed Sun.*

The West Deck

$$ | CARIBBEAN | FAMILY | Opened by the same people who own Pinchos, this fun, friendly, wood-decked grill joint offers casual fare like barbecue ribs and grilled shrimp by the dozen, as well as Caribbean bites like jerk wings, fried *funchi* (like a thick polenta) with Dutch cheese, and West Indian samosas. There are some surprisingly snazzy main dishes, and the signature "Beer-Ritas" (a full bottle of beer served upside down in a big margarita) are legendary. **Known for:** superb sunset views on Surfside Beach; a great pit stop along the Linear Park; eclectic selection of Caribbean fare. ⑤ *Average main: $20* ⊠ *L. G. Smith Blvd., at Governor's Bay, Oranjestad* ☎ *297/587–2667* ⊕ *www.thewestdeck.com.*

Wilhelmina

$$$$ | INTERNATIONAL | Choose from a simple and elegant indoor dining area or a tropical outdoor garden oasis to sample from the creative international menu that includes choices of quality meats, homemade pastas, and fresh fish and seafood, all with suggested wine pairings from the well-regarded cellar. The menu also includes an impressive offering of avant-garde vegetarian dishes. **Known for:** exotic mains like Surinamese sea bass and Indonesian-style roast pork; creative takes on conventional dishes like a signature salad with rock lobster and scallops; excellent selection of fine wines. ⑤ *Average main: $40* ⊠ *Wilhelmenastraat 74, Oranjestad* ☎ *297/583–0445* ⊕ *www.wilhelminaaruba.com* ☾ *Closed Mon. No lunch.*

Coffee and Quick Bites

Chubato Beer World Aruba

$ | INTERNATIONAL | This brand-new spot is owned by the Coffee Break folks, but it's all about a different kind of brew—more than 150 types of beer! Snack platters, sliders, wings, and nachos are also on tap, and they often have live music at night on their sidewalk terrace. **Known for:** lots of wings, and sliders and nachos; 100 types of beer; lively local hangout, sometimes with live music.

⑤ *Average main: $10* ⊠ *Caya G.F Betico Croes 97, Oranjestad* ☎ *297/699–1769* ⊕ *www.facebook.com/ChubatoBeerWorld* ⊙ *Closed Sun.*

Coffee Break

$ | **INTERNATIONAL** | The island's only locally roasted coffee is only available here. They also offer gelato, pastries, soups and sandwiches. **Known for:** fresh modern air-conditioned pit stop; Barista-style concoctions; their own Aruba blend with coconut. ⑤ *Average main: $10* ⊠ *Caya G.F. Betico Croes 101-A, Oranjestad* Ⓜ *Downtown Trolley line.*

The Pastechi House

$ | **CARIBBEAN** | **FAMILY** | Look for the big smiling pastechi sign and a line of locals waiting to grab Aruba's favorite fast food (think empanada), order one for yourself, and wash it down with a cold *batido* (fruit shake). They now have little crab cakes to go as well. **Known for:** popular local pit stop; largest selection of pastechi types; vegan also available. ⑤ *Average main: $10* ⊠ *Caya G. F. Betico Croes 42, Oranjestad* ⊕ *www.facebook.com/thepastechihouse* ⊙ *Closed Sun.* ☞ *Cash only* ▭ *No credit cards* Ⓜ *Downtown Trolley line.*

Hotels

Hyatt Place Aruba Airport

$ | **HOTEL** | Connected directly to the airport by a covered walkway, the contemporary new hotel serves the needs of business and leisure travelers on a budget and is especially convenient for those with flight cancellations. **Pros:** breakfast included with room rate; lovely outdoor pool with bar service; sofa beds in every room make for flexible accommodations. **Cons:** no balconies in any of the rooms; little to do within walking distance; not near a beach. ⑤ *Rooms from: $200* ⊠ *Aruba Airport, Wayaca 6B, Oranjestad* ☎ *297/523–1234* ⊕ *www.hyatt.com* ❤️ *Free Breakfast* ⇥ *116 rooms.*

Renaissance Aruba Ocean Suites

$$$$ | **RESORT** | **FAMILY** | Spacious suites attract families and groups to this downtown resort that offers its own man-made beach on the sea and free water taxi to its lovely private island minutes away. **Pros:** steps from downtown; private island access; spacious water circuit and stellar sea views. **Cons:** limited water sports; limited dining on-site; can be noisy at night as it's right downtown. ⑤ *Rooms from: $543* ⊠ *Renaissance Beach, L. G. Smith Blvd., Oranjestad* ☎ *297/583–6000* ⊕ *www.marriott.com* ⇥ *259 rooms* ❤️ *No Meals.*

Renaissance Aruba Resort and Casino: Marina Hotel

$$$ | HOTEL | The adults-only side of the Aruba Renaissance twin resorts offers guests a chic, waterfront urban oasis in the heart of Downtown with all rooms having been beautifully refreshed and renovated in April 2021. **Pros:** beautiful private island beach with deluxe cabana rentals; good choice of in-hotel nightlife and restaurants and in-house casino; in the heart of the best downtown shopping and dining. **Cons:** marina pool is tiny; rooms are small and have no balconies; nights can be noisy. ⑤ *Rooms from: $464* ✉ *L. G. Smith Blvd. 82, Oranjestad* ☎ *297/583–6000, 800/421–8188* ⊕ *www.marriott.com* ⇆ *296 rooms* ❑ *No Meals.*

🍸 Nightlife

Businesses come and go in the alfresco Renaissance Marketplace on the marina, but it's always lively in the evenings when most of the cafés, bistros, and restaurants transform their vibe with their own live music or entertainment. The sparkling lights on the water and the live bands playing in the common square every evening also add to the magic. This popular gathering spot for locals, as well as visitors, is also the place where you'll find evening pop-up festivals, and there are special events from businesses like Cuba's Cookin and Café the Plaza. But there's also been new nightlife breathed into the back streets directly behind Renaissance Marina Resort with some great new music venues like Hoya Bar in Plaza Daniel Leo, Patio 15 behind Royal Plaza, and further afield across from the cruise terminal, Bochincha Container Yard, which is a massive alfresco food and entertainment gathering spot. And though it's not a bar, the landmark snack spot Djiespie's Place is worth a mention because there's a street party with dancing every Friday night at 6 pm. It's an authentic Aruba night out, and visitors are welcome to join in.

BARS

★ Alfie's in Aruba

PUBS | Owned by a lively expat Canadian couple, this popular watering hole in the back streets of Downtown has been attracting people from all over the world to sample their Canuck-style hospitality and over 50 types of craft beer. Live music Friday Nights also attracts the crowds, and their pub food is to die for. Think seven-cheese Mac 'n' Cheese nights, crispy Nashville style hot fried chicken with a kick, melt-in-your-mouth ribs, and mega-burgers so big you can hardly fit them in your mouth. But they haven't forgotten their homeland; authentic Quebec-style poutine and even vegan poutine are also both available there. Look for the big Canadian flag out front. ✉ *Dominicanessenstraat*

Brewing Up Something Special

Order a "Balashi cocktail" in Aruba only if you want to receive a glass of water. That's because the water purification plant is in Balashi. And don't be afraid to drink the water: it's safe and delicious and made from desalinated seawater. But since the advent of the beer called Balashi—the only beer in the world made from desalinated seawater—you might confuse a barkeep if you order just a "Balashi." Try a Balashi Chill with a wedge of lime in the neck, like many Mexican beers. Keep an eye out for their limited edition brews too like the current Magic Mango; they rotate new ones on a regular basis.

10, Oranjestad ☎ 297/569–5815 ⊕ www.alfiesinaruba.com
⊙ Closed Mon. No lunch.

Apotek Speakeasy

COCKTAIL LOUNGES | It's been a well-kept secret that Aruba has a prohibition-style speakeasy, but now that they're no longer operating as a pop-up, it's much easier for discerning drinkers to find them. Themed like an old-fashioned apothecary—promising to hand-craft potent libations to cure whatever ails you—their dedicated barkeeps are more chemists and mixologists than drink slingers, and really put on a show while using carefully curated ingredients to create complicated libations that impress. The place is tiny, so reservations are a must, but well worth the extra effort if you're a true cocktail connoisseur. ⊠ *Klipstraat 2, Oranjestad* ☎ *297/561–1563* ⊕ *www.apotheekspeakeasy.com* ⊙ *Closed Sun. and Mon.*

★ BLUE

LIVE MUSIC | Located steps away from the cool infinity pool of the Renaissance Marina Hotel, BLUE is one of the hippest social gathering spots on the island. It's the place where young local professionals gather for happy hour during the week. Later it morphs into a hot, nightly DJ-driven scene bathed in blue and violet lights with a giant video wall and talented barkeeps serving upscale concoctions like their signature BLUE Solo Martini. ⊠ *Renaissance Marina Hotel, L. G. Smith Blvd. 82, Oranjestad* ☎ *297/583–6000* ⊕ *www.marriott.com.*

★ Bochincha Container Yard

GATHERING PLACES | An impressive new multistory entertainment complex built from old shipping containers sits right behind the Local Market. The carnival-style atmosphere and high-octane

music provided by either live bands or DJs create the backdrop for an eclectic choice of international fare via food truck–style kiosks; there are also multiple bars, a wine shop, a cigar store, and a tattoo and barber shack. ⊠ *Rockefellerstraat 8* ✛ *Behind the Local Market* ☎ *297/732–0808* ⊕ *bochincha.com* ☉ *No lunch.*

Cafe Chaos

LIVE MUSIC | This is not so much a "dance club" as a place to dance and let loose for mostly local Dutch expats. The no-nonsense bar offers a wide variety of music, from live bands to DJs spanning styles from reggae to funk to rock. It's a mix, and it all depends on the mood of the crowd and the night. But it's a great spot to make new local friends. The live music often starts very late, but you can happen upon some crazy jam sessions, too. ⊠ *L. G. Smith Blvd. 60, Oranjestad* ☎ *297/588–7547* ⊕ *www.facebook. com/chaosaruba.*

5 o'Clock Somewhere Bar and Grill

BARS | Though this massive circular alfresco bar in the middle of Renaissance Marketplace might resemble Jimmy Buffet's Margaritaville, it's not part of the franchise though it certainly evokes the same vibe with two daily happy hours. Think large frozen tropical cocktails, island music, and typical beach bar fare like wings, tacos, and burgers. Surprisingly, it's also a great spot to try some locally inspired fare like snack platters of pastechi and Dutch krokets, and individual portions of keshi yena which is considered Aruba's national dish. ⊠ *Renaissance Marketplace, L.G. Smith Blvd. 82, Oranjestad* ☎ *297/523–6782* ⊕ *www.facebook. com/5somewherearuba.*

★ Hoya Lush Cafe

COCKTAIL LOUNGES | This sophisticated alfresco emporium has totally transformed the courtyard of Plaza Daniel Leo into an exciting gathering spot offering up cool tapas like Argentinian artisanal empanadas and a large selection of killer creative handcrafted cocktails and sangrias; it's also a champagne and wine bar. There's a cheery tropical vibe by day and a cool outdoor lounge vibe at night but on weekends it goes full-on electric with neon lighting shows and trendy music. Beyond the bar and tables there are also oversized lounging swings if you want to imbibe in style. Daily happy hour is 4–6 pm. ⊠ *Plaza Daniel Leo Oranjestad, Oranjestad* ☎ *297/562–3515* ⊕ *www.facebook.com/hoyalush.*

Lucy's Retired Surfers Bar & Restaurant

It may not be on the beach, but Lucy's has the quintessential beach bar vibe and there is a small man-made beach area outside replete with hammocks. By day it's a lunch spot serving up

burgers and hearty American fare, but it ramps up the vibe at happy hour and then becomes a hot nightlife spot later with live music and creative drink specials. They are also one of Aruba's only officially dog-friendly bars. ⊠ *Renaissance Marina, L. G. Smith Blvd. 82, Oranjestad* ☎ *297/280–1970* ⊕ *www.lucyssurf.com.*

Umbrella Lounge Aruba

BARS | Look for the colorful collection of upside-down umbrellas across from Fort Zoutman to find this cool new bar and grill that offers a myriad of vibes depending on the time of day. Most folks enjoy the great local food like ribs and fish cakes with creole sauce while socializing at the outdoor tables, while the ultra-modern bar inside seems the place for serious partying and watching sports on the giant screens. But later, it's all about dancing inside and out once the DJ starts spinning the tunes in sync with the laser light show from the elevated stage. ⊠ *Zoutmanstraat 7, Oranjestad* ☎ *297/561–7404* ⊕ *umbrellaloungearuba.business.site.*

★ The West Deck Island Grill Beach Bar

Just over the wooden walkway from Renaissance Ocean Suites along the Linear Park you'll find this casual wooden deck beach bar on the water that's called Governor's Bay. Enjoy one of their special upside-down margaritas or incredible craft cocktails while you catch a stellar sunset and watch the cruise ships go by. After dark, the music takes it up a notch—sometimes live—and the atmosphere is fun and friendly. It's as popular with locals as it is with visitors. Great Caribbean tapas and grilled specialties are also on tap. ⊠ *Governor's Bay Oranjestad, L. G. Smith Blvd., Oranjestad* ✛ *Linear Park (next to the Queen Wilhelmina Park, adjacent to the Renaissance Suites)* ☎ *297/587–2667* ⊕ *www. thewestdeck.com.*

WEEKLY PARTIES

★ Bon Bini Festival

FESTIVALS | This year-round folklore event (the name means "welcome" in Papiamento) is held every Tuesday from 6:30 pm to 8:30 pm at Ft. Zoutman in Oranjestad. In the inner courtyard, you can check out the Antillean dancers in resplendent costumes, feel the rhythms of the steel drums, browse among the stands displaying local artwork, and sample local food and drink. ⊠ *Fort Zoutman, Oranjestad* ⊕ *www.aruba.com* ▣ *$5.*

🎭 Performing Arts

Aruba has a handful of not-so-famous but very talented performers. Over the years, several local artists, including composer Julio Renado Euson, choreographer Wilma Kuiperi, sculptor Ciro Abath,

This popular photo-op spot can be found in downtown Oranjestad.

and visual artist Elvis Lopez, have gained international renown. Furthermore, many Aruban musicians play more than one type of music (classical, jazz, soca, salsa, reggae, calypso, rap, pop), and many compose as well as perform. Edjean Semeleer has followed in the footsteps of his mentor Padu Lampe—the composer of the island's national anthem and a beloved local star—to become one of the island's best-loved entertainers. His performances pack Aruba's biggest halls, especially his annual Christmas concert. He sings in many languages, and though he's young, his style is old-style crooner—Aruba's answer to Michael Bublé.

Cas Di Cultura
ARTS CENTERS | The National Theater of Aruba, the island's cultural center, hosts art exhibits, folkloric shows, dance performances, and concerts throughout the year. ⊠ *Stichting Shouwburg Aruba, Vondellaan 2, Oranjestad* ☎ *297/582–1010* ⊕ *www.casdicultura.aw.*

UNOCA
ARTS CENTERS | Although UNOCA is Aruba's national gallery, it's much more, acting as an anchor to host cultural and performance events, which are often held there. ⊠ *Stadionweg 21, Oranjestad* ☎ *297/583–5681* ⊕ *unoca.aw.*

ANNUAL ARTS FESTIVALS
The island's many festivals showcase arts and culture on a rotating basis with new ones popping up all the time. To find out what's going on, check out the local English-language newspapers or look for events online at www.aruba.com/us/calendar.

🛍 Shopping

Oranjestad's original "Main Street" (behind the Renaissance Marina Resort) has seen a massive renovation of the entire downtown region, which has breathed new life into the backstreets, adding pedestrian-only stretches, compact malls, and open resting areas. A free ecotrolley now loops throughout downtown, allowing you to hop on and off to shop and stroll. Stores selling fashions, souvenirs, specialty items, sporting goods, and cosmetics can all be found on this renewed street, along with plenty of cafés, snack spots, and outdoor terraces.

CIGARS

Cigar Emporium

TOBACCO | The Cubans come straight from the climate-controlled humidor at Cigar Emporium. Choose from Cohiba, Montecristo, Romeo y Julieta, Partagas, and more. ⊠ *Renaissance Mall, L. G. Smith Blvd. 82, Oranjestad* 🕾 *297/582–5479* ⊕ *www.facebook. com/cigaremporiumaruba* 🕙 *Closed Sun.*

DUTY-FREE STORES

Dufry

JEWELRY & WATCHES | No doubt you've seen this brand of duty-free stores in airports all over the world, but don't expect to see the same duty-free items like tobacco and spirits in this one, and the prices are not completely duty-free. What you will find are great bargains on cosmetics, perfumes, jewelry, and accessories from such brands as Carolina Herrera, Calvin Klein, Armani, Montblanc, and more. And there's always some kind of major sale on something of good quality going on there. There's another outlet in Royal Plaza Mall. ⊠ *G. F. Betico Croes 29, Oranjestad* 🕾 *297/582–2790* ⊕ *www.dufry.com* 🕙 *Closed Sun.*

ELECTRONICS

★ Boolchand's Digital World

ELECTRONICS | Family-run Boolchand's began in the 1930s and has since become a major retail institution throughout the Caribbean; they opened their first shop on Aruba in 1974. Today, their downtown "Digital World" is your one-stop shop to get a high-tech fix at seriously low prices. Top-quality merchandise by major brands includes the latest in computers, cameras, and tech accessories, as well as quality watches and Pandora jewelry. ⊠ *Havenstraat 25, Oranjestad* 🕾 *297/583–0147* ⊕ *boolchand.com* 🕙 *Closed Sun.*

FOOD

Ling & Sons IGA Super Center

SUPERMARKET | Always a family-owned and-operated grocery company, Ling and Sons adopted the IGA-brand supermarket-style

with all the goods you would expect in an IGA back home. In addition to a wide variety of foods, there's a bakery, a deli, a butcher shop, and a well-stocked "liquortique." You can also order your groceries online to be delivered to your hotel room. ■ TIP➜ **Ask about their VIP card for discounts and note that the store closes at 3 pm.** ⊠ *Schotlandstraat 41, Oranjestad* ☎ *297/521–2370* ⊕ *www. lingandsons.com* ⊗ *Closed Sun.*

GIFTS AND SOUVENIRS

★ Designs of Color by Dariana

ART GALLERIES | It's impossible not to be stopped in your tracks walking by this new art boutique in the Renaissance Marketplace due to the stunning original pieces showcased in the window. The thoughtfully curated and colorful collection of one-of-a-kind resin art sculptures and art pieces are not only ideal souvenirs, but also make wonderful top quality gifts. ⊠ *Renaissance Marketplace, L. G. Smith Blvd. 9, Oranjestad* ☎ *297/568–6283* ⊗ *Closed Sun.*

★ The Mask—Mopa Mopa Art

CRAFTS | These shops specialize in original masks and crafty items called mopa mopa art. Originating with the Quillacingas people of Ecuador and Colombia, the art is made from the bud of the mopa mopa tree, boiled down into a resin, colored with dyes, and applied to carved mahogany and other woods like cedar. Masks, jewelry boxes, coasters, whimsical animal figurines, and more make wonderfully unique gifts and souvenirs. The masks are also believed to ward off evil spirits. Find them in Paseo Herencia Mall, Royal Plaza Mall, Renaissance Marketplace and Alhambra Mall. You can also buy works online. ⊠ *Renaissance Marketplace, L. G. Smith Blvd. 9, Oranjestad* ☎ *297/588–7297* ⊕ *www.mopamopaaruba.com* ⊗ *Closed Sun.*

JEWELRY

★ Colombian Emeralds International

JEWELRY & WATCHES | A trusted international jewelry dealer specializing in emeralds, this outlet also has a top-notch selection of diamonds, sapphire, tanzanite, rubies, ammolite, pearls, gold, semiprecious gems, luxury watches, and more at very competitive prices. A highly professional and knowledgeable staff adds to their credibility. (They also have a duty-free store in the airport.) ⊠ *Renaissance Mall, L. G. Smith Blvd. 82, Oranjestad* ☎ *297/583– 6238* ⊕ *www.colombianemeralds.com.*

Gandelman Jewelers

JEWELRY & WATCHES | Established in 1936, this family-run store is one of the island's premier jewelers. It's also Aruba's official Rolex retailer and the exclusive agent for names like Cartier (the only official retailer on the island), Patek Philippe, and David Yurman.

There are two other stores on Aruba in the Aruba Marriott and the Aruba Hyatt Regency in addition to this flagship. ⊠ *Renaissance Mall, L. G. Smith Blvd. 82, Oranjestad* ☎ *297/529–9920* ⊕ *www. gandelman.net* ⊙ *Closed Sun.*

★ Kay's Fine Jewelry
JEWELRY & WATCHES | Kay's family-run emporium is a well-known Aruba fixture on the fine-jewelry scene, and their designs have won awards. Exquisite settings featuring white and colored diamonds are their claim to fame, and they also have a fine selection of precious gems and brand-name timepieces. ⊠ *Westraat 8, Oranjestad* ☎ *297/588–9978* ⊕ *www.kaysfinejewelry.com* ⊙ *Closed Sun.*

Little Switzerland
With stores in the Royal Plaza Mall and one in Paseo Herencia—these well-known outlets specialize in designer jewelry and upscale timepieces by big-name designers like TAG Heuer, David Yurman, Breitling, Roberto Coin, Chopard, Pandora, Tiffany & Co., Cartier, Movado, Omega, and John Hardy. They also own the TAG Heuer Boutique in the Renaissance Mall. ⊠ *Royal Plaza Mall, L. G. Smith Blvd. 94, Oranjestad* ☎ *248/809–5560 ext. 40230* ⊕ *www. littleswitzerland.com.*

MALLS AND MARKETPLACES
The Local Market Aruba
MARKET | Focusing on locally made or inspired ware, this large outdoor flea market across from the cruise terminal offers great deals on paintings, local music, cigars, sunglasses, local handicrafts, souvenirs and more, and the food trucks on-site are excellent. It closes at 6 pm. ⊠ *Between Paardenbaaistraat and Rockefellerstraat, in front of the cruise terminal, Oranjestad* ☎ *297/733–1982* ⊕ *www.facebook.com/thelocalmarketaruba/.*

★ Renaissance Mall
MALL | Upscale, name-brand fashion and luxury brands of perfume, cosmetics, and leather goods are what you'll find in the array of 60 stores spanning two floors in this mall located within and underneath the Renaissance Marina Resort. You'll also find specialty items like cigars and designer shoes plus high-end gold, silver, diamonds, and quality jewelry at low- or no-duty prices. Cafés and high-end dining, plus a casino and spa, round out the offerings. Shopping until 7 pm daily. ⊠ *Renaissance Marina Resort, L. G. Smith Blvd. 82, Oranjestad* ☎ *297/523–6065* ⊕ *www.shoprenaissancearuba.com* ⊙ *Closed Sun.*

★ Renaissance Marketplace
MALL | FAMILY | The Renaissance Marketplace is more of a dining and gathering spot along the marina than a market, though they

do hold a weekly local artisan's outdoor market every Friday night. It's a lively spot with a few souvenir shops and specialty stores, and locals frequent the modern cinema. But mostly it's full of eclectic dining emporiums and trendy cafés, and they have live music some weekends in their alfresco square. The Wind Creek Seaport casino is also there, and it's steps from the cruise terminal on the marina. ⊠ *L. G. Smith Blvd. 82, Oranjestad* ☎ *297/583–6000* ⊕ *www.shoprenaissancearuba.com.*

Royal Plaza Mall

MALL | It's impossible to miss this gorgeous colonial-style, cotton-candy-colored building with the big gold dome gracing the front street along the marina. It's one of the most photographed in Oranjestad. Three levels of shops (both indoors and out) make up this artsy arcade full of small boutiques, cigar shops, designer clothing outlets, gift and jewelry stores, and souvenir kiosks. Great dining and bars are found within as well. ⊠ *L. G. Smith Blvd. 94, Oranjestad* ☎ *297/588–0351* ☽ *Closed Sun.*

PERFUMES AND COSMETICS

Penha, Dufry, Little Switzerland, and Maggy's are all known for their extensive fragrance offerings.

Penha

SOUVENIRS | Originating in Curaçao in 1865, Penha has branched out throughout the Caribbean and has eight stores on Aruba. The largest is right next to the Renaissance Marina Hotel. The store is particularly known for good prices on high-end perfumes, cosmetics, skin-care products, eyewear, and fashions. You'll find brand names such as MAC, Lancôme, Estée Lauder, Clinique, Chanel, Dior, Montblanc, and Victoria's Secret to name just a few. There's another location in Palm Beach Plaza. ⊠ *Caya G. F. Betico Croes 11/13, Oranjestad* ☎ *297/582–0082* ⊕ *www.jlpenha.com.*

SPAS

Okeanos Spa

SPAS | The full-service spa at the Renaissance Marina Hotel is well equipped to help you relax to the max, but the incredible seaside palapa cove on private Renaissance Island is the best venue for a relaxing massage or treatment. It's accessible by free water taxi when you book a treatment, and your purchase also gains you access to the stellar protected coves and white-sand beaches. Access to the island is otherwise limited to Renaissance guests. There is a beach bar and a full-service restaurant on-site, so you can make an entire blissful day of it. ⊠ *Renaissance Aruba Resort & Casino, L. G. Smith Blvd. 82, Oranjestad* ☎ *297/583–6000* ⊕ *www.renaissancearubaspa.com.*

MANCHEBO, DRUIF, AND EAGLE BEACHES

Updated by
Susan Campbell

👁 **Sights** 🍴 **Restaurants** 🛏 **Hotels** 🛍 **Shopping** 🍸 **Nightlife**

★★★☆☆   ★★★★☆   ★★★★★   ★★☆☆☆   ★★☆☆☆

NEIGHBORHOOD SNAPSHOT

TOP EXPERIENCES

■ **Stroll Silky Sand:** Take long walks along a carpet of white sand capped with fiery sunsets.

■ **Dine Out in Style:** There's an eclectic array of unique dining locations: barefoot on the beach, canopied beds, or an intimate chef's table.

■ **Pamper Body and Soul:** Join beach-front yoga classes or partake in luxurious seaside massages.

■ **Dance Under the Stars:** Head to Alhambra Mall and Casino for live music at the alfresco restaurants and bars.

■ **Golf with Nature:** Play a picturesque round of golf amid ocean-view greens and beautifully landscaped lagoons.

GETTING HERE AND AROUND

The Eagle Beach region—also known as the low-rise section—is actually three beaches connected to each other, beginning right between the tip of downtown Oranjestad just past the cruise-ship terminal and ending at the Bubali wetlands just before the Divi Aruba Phoenix. It's about a 15- to 20-minute drive from the airport and it's accessible by public bus from the downtown terminal. There's free parking along the beaches.

PLANNING YOUR TIME

The best time to visit is during the day if you're seeking beach fun. There's no real nightlife, and except for the parties and entertainment for guests at the resorts, the Alhambra Mall and Casino is the only lively public place at night.

VIEWFINDER

■ Of course, the most iconic photo in this region is the emblematic Fofoti tree on Eagle Beach, but anywhere along that stretch will give you an ideal backdrop for your "I'm finally here in paradise" pics. At **Divi's BeachBar** on Druif Beach, you can get a ringside seat to the antics of the lively seabirds diving for fish at the "pelican poles." The picturesque poles are remnants of the old Eagle Refinery dock and the birds love to perch on them; it's also an enchanting spot for dramatic "sunset over the sea" shots.

Unlike the action-packed party that is Palm Beach, Eagle Beach is where you go to unwind, relax, recharge, and rejuvenate in pristine postcard-perfect settings. Once you experience it, you'll see why it's consistently rated among the top three beaches on the planet, and you'll want to go back.

Nearby, an entire village of Divi Resorts encompasses Druif Beach, while Manchebo Beach is the broadest stretch of sand on the island. It's become the spot for health and wellness retreats, and it's known to have the most eco-friendly hotel in the entire Caribbean.

👁 Sights

There are few attractions or historic sites in this area. Pastimes are purely sun-and-sand–oriented with sunset strolls and toes-in-the-sand dining entertainment, enough for those who choose to stay in the low-rise region; activities typically center around the respective resorts.

The area's most famous sight is the iconic Fofoti tree on Eagle Beach. It's the island's most photographed tree, and the one that you so often see in Aruba's marketing and promotions; it's often mistakenly referred to as a divi-divi tree, and though similar, they are not the same species.

★ Gloria-Movies, Entertainment, Dining & Play

PERFORMANCE VENUE | This exciting new entertainment complex was named after "Teatro Gloria," Aruba's very first movie theatre built back in 1930s, and now offers the most modern cinematic experience in the entire Caribbean. There are ten cinemas in all including IMAX and VIP Theatres and there's also a children's bouncy playground, a Starbucks, a huge food court, and stand-alone upscale dining options like P.F. Chang's and VIP Grill & Lounge. There are also special musical events with live bands or DJs. ✉ Caya Dr. J.E.M. Arends 8, Eagle Beach ☎ 297/523–6841 ⊕ www.facebook.com/TheMoviesIMAXGloria.

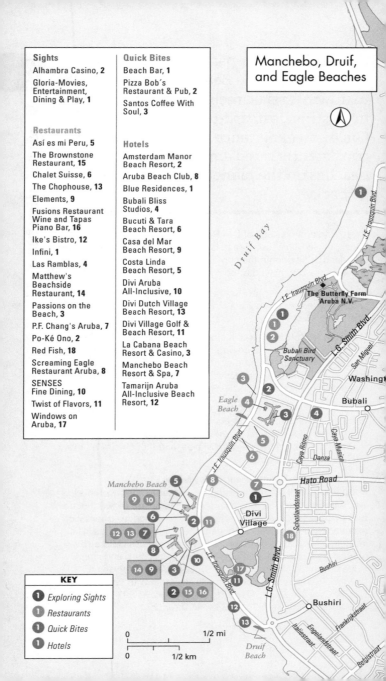

Manchebo, Druif, and Eagle Beaches

Sights

Alhambra Casino, **2**

Gloria-Movies, Entertainment, Dining & Play, **1**

Restaurants

Así es mi Peru, **5**

The Brownstone Restaurant, **15**

Chalet Suisse, **6**

The Chophouse, **13**

Elements, **9**

Fusions Restaurant Wine and Tapas Piano Bar, **16**

Ike's Bistro, **12**

Infini, **1**

Las Ramblas, **4**

Matthew's Beachside Restaurant, **14**

Passions on the Beach, **3**

P.F. Chang's Aruba, **7**

Po-Ké Ono, **2**

Red Fish, **18**

Screaming Eagle Restaurant Aruba, **8**

SENSES Fine Dining, **10**

Twist of Flavors, **11**

Windows on Aruba, **17**

Quick Bites

Beach Bar, **1**

Pizza Bob's Restaurant & Pub, **2**

Santos Coffee With Soul, **3**

Hotels

Amsterdam Manor Beach Resort, **2**

Aruba Beach Club, **8**

Blue Residences, **1**

Bubali Bliss Studios, **4**

Bucuti & Tara Beach Resort, **6**

Casa del Mar Beach Resort, **9**

Costa Linda Beach Resort, **5**

Divi Aruba All-Inclusive, **10**

Divi Dutch Village Beach Resort, **13**

Divi Village Golf & Beach Resort, **11**

La Cabana Beach Resort & Casino, **3**

Manchebo Beach Resort & Spa, **7**

Tamarijn Aruba All-Inclusive Beach Resort, **12**

KEY

- ⓵ Exploring Sights
- ⓵ Restaurants
- ⓵ Quick Bites
- ⓵ Hotels

Druif Bay

The Butterfly Farm Aruba N.V.

Bubali Bird Sanctuary

Eagle Beach

Manchebo Beach

Divi Village

J.E. Irausquin Blvd.

L.G. Smith Blvd.

San Miguel

Washington

Bubali

Caya Ritmo

Danza

Caya Musica

Hato Road

Schotlandstraat

Bushiri

Bushiri

Druif Beach

Engelandstraat

Italiestraat

Frankrijkstraat

Belgiestraat

0   1/2 mi

0   1/2 km

CASINOS

⭐ Alhambra Casino

CASINO | Part of the Divi family and accessible by golf cart from the company's all-inclusive resorts, this is a lively popular casino with a big selection of modern slots, blackjack, craps, poker, roulette, and more. Be sure to join their Player's Club—it's free and offers free slot credits, and you earn points with your card as well. The Cove restaurant serves light meals and drinks; you'll also receive free drinks on the floor when you're playing the games. Special theme nights and promotions run all week, and Super Bingo is Thursday, Friday, and Saturday afternoons. ⊠ *L. G. Smith Blvd. 47, Druif* ☎ *297/588–9000* ⊕ *www.casinoalhambra.com.*

 Beaches

Aruba's low-rise region is lined with beautiful beaches. Some have adopted the names of the resorts they are famous for: Manchebo Beach is technically the beginning of Eagle Beach, and Divi Beach is still Druif Beach, named for the type of trees that used to grow in abundance there. They join at Punta Brabo, which means rough point, and it's aptly named as the current and rip tides there can be severe and there's a quick drop-off. Eagle Beach continues in a long straight line afterward, and has often been named one of the world's top three beaches for good reason. Surf is usually gentle, but it can be occasionally rough too, so heed the warning flags as there are no lifeguards.

Druif Beach

BEACH | Fine white sand and calm water make this beach a great choice for sunbathing and swimming. It's the base beach for the Divi collections of all-inclusive resorts, so amenities are reserved for guests. But the locals like it, too, and often camp out here as well with their own chairs and coolers. The beach is accessible by bus, rental car, or taxi, and it's within easy walking distance to many stores for food and drinks. The new Beach Bar—owned by Divi Resorts, but not part of the all-inclusive plan—is open to the public and a superb spot to have lunch or early dinner, swim, and watch the sunset. **Amenities:** food and drink; toilets; parking (free); water sports. **Best for:** swimming; partiers. ⊠ *J. E. Irausquin Blvd., Druif* ⊕ *Near the Divi resorts, south of Punta Brabo.*

⭐ Eagle Beach

BEACH | Aruba's most photographed stretch of sand, Eagle Beach is not only a favorite with visitors and locals, but also of sea turtles. More sea turtles nest here than anywhere else on the island. This pristine stretch of blinding white sand and aqua surf is ranked among the best beaches in the world. Many of the hotels have

Did You Know?

Hurricanes don't always cause beach erosion. When Hurricane Ivan passed north of Aruba in 2004 (one of the rare hurricanes that directly affected the island), Eagle Beach actually got a few feet wider.

facilities on or near the beach, and refreshments are never far away, but chairs and shade palapas are reserved for resort guests only. **Amenities:** food and drink; toilets; parking (no fee). **Best for:** sunsets; swimming; water sports. ⊠ *J. E. Irausquin Blvd., north of Manchebo Beach, Druif.*

★ Manchebo Beach (*Punta Brabo*)

BEACH | Impressively wide, the white-sand shoreline in front of the Manchebo Beach Resort (technically where Eagle Beach begins) is the backdrop for the numerous yoga classes now taking place under the giant palapa since the resort began offering health and wellness retreats. This sandy stretch is the broadest on the island; in fact you can even get a workout just getting to the water! Waves can be rough and wild at certain times of the year, though, so mind the current and undertow when swimming. **Amenities:** food and drink; toilets. **Best for:** swimming; sunsets; walking. ■ TIP→ **The Bucuti beach bar is reserved exclusively for guests of the** *Bucuti & Tara Beach Resort.* ⊠ *J. E. Irausquin Blvd., Druif* ✛ *At Manchebo Beach Resort.*

Restaurants

The Eagle Beach region has an eclectic selection of dining options from high-end eateries to romantic private dining options and friendly beach bar haunts for burgers and barbecue. Many of the finest spots are part of a resort and are open to the public, but there are a few excellent stand-alone exceptions.

Asi es mi Peru

$$$ | PERUVIAN | Owner Roxanna Salinas has created an authentic Peruvian-style dining spot to share a taste of her home with locals and visitors alike. Authentic specialties are artfully served in a warm and colorful enclave, and a portion of proceeds from the wares sold at the on-site Peruvian craft market go to a local Aruban cancer foundation as well. **Known for:** five-course chef's table sampling menu on request; Peruvian-style ceviche made table-side; vegetarian and vegan menu available. ⑤ *Average main: $26* ⊠ *Paradise Beach Villas, J. E. Irausquin Blvd. 64, Eagle Beach* ☎ *297/525–4000 ext. 172* ⊕ *www.asiesmiperuenaruba.com* ☉ *Closed Mon.*

The Brownstone Restaurant

$$$ | INTERNATIONAL | The latest hip spot in Alhambra Mall was fashioned after a New York-style lounge, steak house, and sports bar with a focus on good stiff drinks, great steaks, and hearty portions of ribs, chicken, and fish. Pretentious it's not, but the fare is first-rate, and they have a well-curated selection of creative

cocktails using only top-quality spirits. **Known for:** friendly, welcoming atmosphere and service; all-you-can eat ribs on Saturdays; signature 16-ounce T-Bone steaks. $ *Average main: $25* ⊠ *Alhambra Mall, J.E Irausquin Blvd. 47, Manchebo Beach* ☎ 297/280–7500 ⊕ *www.facebook.com/BROWNSTONEARUBA* ⊗ *No lunch.*

Chalet Suisse
$$$$ | **EUROPEAN** | Opened in 1988 as a re-created Swiss-style chalet, this is a perennial favorite for the time-share folks and repeat visitors due to its high-quality classic European dishes—chicken cordon bleu, beef Stroganoff, and duck à l'orange—as well as island-inspired favorites like stuffed, locally caught grouper medallions. They also have rotating seasonally inspired menus, and their low season early-bird menu is very popular. **Known for:** excellent wine cellar; expertly prepared whole rack of lamb; rich Swiss chocolate fondue for dessert. $ *Average main: $40* ⊠ *J. E. Irausquin Blvd. 246, Eagle Beach* ☎ 297/587–5054 ⊕ *www. chaletsuisse-aruba.com* ⊗ *Closed Sun. No lunch.*

★ The Chophouse
$$$$ | **INTERNATIONAL** | Low-key elegance and soft piano music set the stage for this indoor enclave where meaty chops and steaks are king and classic silver service is still in vogue. The big surprise here though is the chic Omakase Japanese Sushi Bar that shares the space, and their selection of vegetarian, vegan, and gluten-free options is impressive. **Known for:** elegant old-world atmosphere combined with a modern sushi bar; premium steaks and chops; predominately organic and sustainable fare. $ *Average main: $45* ⊠ *Manchebo Resort, J. E. Irausquin Blvd. 55, Druif* ☎ 297/522–3444 ⊕ *www.thechophousearuba.com* ⊗ *Sushi bar closed Sun. and Mon.*

★ Elements
$$$$ | **CONTEMPORARY** | A stellar spot with stunning seaside views, this strictly adults-only dining spot embodies the resort's global reputation for promoting green living and a healthy lifestyle. The wide-ranging menu of internationally flavored dishes includes many organic, vegan, vegetarian, and gluten-free choices that use locally sourced ingredients whenever possible. **Known for:** romantic surfside atmosphere with private prix-fixe palapa dining for two; a la carte Sunday Brunch also available for take-out; excellent selection of wines, winner of the Wine Spectator Award of Excellence 2021. $ *Average main: $40* ⊠ *Bucuti and Tara Beach Resort, L. G. Smith Blvd. 55B, Eagle Beach* ☎ 297/583–1100 ⊕ *www. elementsaruba.com* ☞ *Credit cards only, no cash.*

★ Fusions Restaurant Wine and Tapas Piano Bar

$$$$ | INTERNATIONAL | What began as a classy laid-back wine and tapas piano bar, has evolved into more of a New York-style steak lounge meets BBQ joint thanks to the popularity of the Big Green Egg BBQ trend. Once they began using this ceramic outdoor charcoal grill to offer up big hearty juicy cowboy steaks and grilled lobster tails, the aroma and smoke drew an entirely different kind of hungry and hearty crowd. **Known for:** Fusions special for two (22-oz. Cowboy steak, two lobster tails, and wine); creative "pair and share" tapas selections; excellent selection of wine. ⑤ *Average main: $45 ⊠ Alhambra Mall, J.E. Irausquin Blvd., Druif ☎ 297/280–9994 ⊕ www.fusion-aruba.com ⊙ Closed Sun. No lunch.*

★ Ike's Bistro

$$$ | INTERNATIONAL | Completely reimagined in 2018 as a contemporary poolside dining option at Manchebo Resort, the new menus and special nights are attracting people seeking inspired Caribbean-international cuisine, and vegans are especially excited about an entire menu devoted to gourmet plant-based dining. Creative preparations of meat, seafood, and fish—locally sourced whenever possible—are all enhanced with flavors from the on-site fresh herb garden, and the chef often surprises with exotic daily specials. **Known for:** four-course chef's surprise tasting menu, with or without wine; paella night Thursday with Spanish music and live cooking; lobster night Monday. ⑤ *Average main: $30 ⊠ Manchebo Beach Resort, J. E. Irausquin Blvd. 55, Druif ☎ 297/522–3444 ⊕ www.ikesbistro.com.*

★ Infini

$$$$ | FUSION | Created in spring 2021 by legendary local chef Urvin Croes, one of the island's most innovative purveyors of ultra-modern cuisine, this new chef's table experience offers infinite possibilities for the palate. The "Chef's Impression" experience is an extensive 8-course themed menu based on world flavors and seasonal, locally sourced (whenever possible) ingredients; the plating of each dish is often so exquisite you might hesitate to dig in, but don't. **Known for:** vegan or dietary restriction menus available with advance notice; chef and team personally talk you through the dining journey; wine and craft cocktail pairings for an extra charge. ⑤ *Average main: $139 ⊠ J.E. Irausquin Blvd. 266, Eagle Beach ☎ 297/280–8869, 297/699–3982 ⊕ infiniaruba.com ⊙ Closed Mon. No lunch.*

Las Ramblas

$$$ | SPANISH | This small alfresco Spanish-theme restaurant at La Cabana is often off-radar for anyone that's not a guest at the resort, but it's worth seeking out for excellent charcoal-grilled

steaks and chops and superb seafood paella. And, even though it's not right on the water, you still can view stunning sunsets from its perch across the road from Eagle Beach. **Known for:** soft live guitar music and tiki torches make the setting very romantic; good selection of Spanish wines and homemade sangrias; excellent classic service. $ *Average main: $30* ⊠ *La Cabana Beach Resort, J. E. Irausquin Blvd. 250, Eagle Beach* ☎ *297/520–1100* ⊕ *www. lacabana.com* ⊗ *Closed Sun. No lunch.*

Matthew's Beachside Restaurant

$$$ | INTERNATIONAL | The lively seaside eatery is popular with nonguests who make a special trip to enjoy great food (meats, fish, seafood, and a good selection of Italian specialties), superb sunsets, and the warm camaraderie of fun folks. It's a great place to catch the game or enjoy happy-hour specials and snacks, and they serve breakfast and lunch, too. **Known for:** Friday wine and tapas nights; all-you-can-eat-ribs Tuesday; prix-fixe early bird menu (except Tues.). $ *Average main: $30* ⊠ *Casa del Mar, J. E. Irausquin Blvd. 51, Manchebo Beach* ☎ *297/588–7300* ⊕ *www. matthews-aruba.com.*

Passions on the Beach

$$$$ | INTERNATIONAL | With stunning seafront sunsets and tiki torch lighting to enhance the mood, the signature restaurant of Amsterdam Manor is a favorite romantic escape for those seeking toes-in-the-sand dining. Popular with families (children under three eat free) and small groups as well, beachfront breakfasts and lunches are served, and though "reef cuisine" is their specialty, there's also meat, vegetarian, and vegan offerings. **Known for:** romantic toes-in-the-sand dining; signature seafood platters; three-course prix-fixe menu. $ *Average main: $45* ⊠ *Amsterdam Manor Beach Resort, J. E. Irausquin Blvd. 252, Eagle Beach* ☎ *800/527–1118* ⊕ *www.passions-restaurant-aruba.com* ☞ *Credit or debit cards only, no cash.*

P.F. Chang's Aruba

$$ | ASIAN | Arubans were delighted to welcome this massive indoor/outdoor eatery promising "elevated Asian cuisine" as the flagship dining spot of the Gloria entertainment venue, and it delivers. Especially popular for special occasions and family-style dinners, it's also a good spot for pre- or post-cinema meals, and their "Vibrant Sundays" from 3–6 pm features live or DJ-driven music. **Known for:** an eclectic selection of dim sum, handmade sushi, wok-fired bowls, and Asian-style noodles; all dishes made-from scratch with fresh ingredients; specialties from China, Japan, Korea, Thailand and beyond. $ *Average main: $20* ⊠ *Caya Dr. J.E.M. Arends 1, Eagle Beach* ☎ *297/523–6832* ⊕ *pfchangsaruba.aw.*

Po-Ké Ono

$$ | ASIAN | Tucked away in the lobby of Azure Residences on Eagle Beach, this is another culinary venture by legendary Chef Urvin Croes (owner of Infini), but here Croes strays from high-end upscale modern cuisine to creative Asian comfort food. His fresh takes on poke, sushi, and steamed baos are inspired by his Chinese heritage; he also offers up some delicious vegan versions as well. **Known for:** unique morning treats like Thai breakfast bowls and Asian omelets; authentic Hawaiian spam poké; hoisin pork belly baos. $ *Average main: $15* ⊠ *Azure Residences, J.E. Irausquin Blvd. 266, Eagle Beach* ☎ *297/525–3610* ⊕ *pokeonoaruba.com* ☻ *Closed Sun.*

Red Fish

$$ | CARIBBEAN | The owners of the legendary downtown restaurant Driftwood and its sister operation Driftwood Fishing Charters opened this much smaller and far less formal dining nook centered around fresh fish and seafood. Locals love it and visitors are just beginning to discover it. **Known for:** fresh fish and seafood by the pound; seafood pastas and paella; authentic local experience. $ *Average main: $15* ⊠ *Orange Plaza, Italiestraat 50, Druif* ✛ *On the road directly behind the Divi golf course* ☎ *297/280–6666* ⊕ *www.redfisharuba.com* ☻ *Closed Mon.*

★ Screaming Eagle Restaurant Aruba

$$$$ | INTERNATIONAL | Not content to perch on its laurels being one of the most consistently highest-rated dining spots on the island, Screaming Eagle decided to reinvent itself recently to offer a more enticing alfresco experience by creating a toes-in-the sand dining experience without actually being at the beach! Thankfully, they haven't messed with the food, still serving up killer international fare, with an extensive wine list to match. **Known for:** excellent wine cellar and multiple Wine Spectator awards; excellent and eclectic selection of fresh fish and seafood dishes as well as top quality meats; rotating menu of seasonal specialties and three-course surprise menu also available in vegetarian and vegan versions. $ *Average main: $45* ⊠ *J. E. Irausquin Blvd. 228, Eagle Beach* ☎ *297/566–3050* ⊕ *screamingeaglearuba.com* ☻ *No lunch.*

SENSES Fine Dining

$$$$ | INTERNATIONAL | Secreted away on the Bucuti & Tara Beach Resort property is an independently operated chef's table experience that features an ever-changing menu with nods to classic French cooking techniques combined with Dutch, Norwegian, and Indonesian influences that fuse into exceptional and often surprising creations. The unique eight-course culinary adventure includes a welcome toast of prosecco and optional curated wine

pairing per dish, plus there's an extensive bottled wine list, craft beer selection, and creative signature cocktails. **Known for:** an exciting luxury brunch experience; a fun and informative culinary adventure; modern fusion cuisine. ⑤ *Average main: $110* ✉ *Bucuti & Tara Beach Resort, J.E. Irausquin Blvd 55B, Eagle Beach* ☎ *297/586–0044* ⊕ *sensesaruba.restaurant.*

★ Twist of Flavors

$$$ | **INTERNATIONAL** | **FAMILY** | There's always something cool happening at this bright and lively indoor-outdoor spot on the corner of Alhambra Mall. The internationally kaleidoscopic menu includes everything from Dutch pancakes to Asian specialties to gourmet burgers to Caribbean seafood, pasta, and more…and surprisingly, they do it all very well. **Known for:** specials nights like Friday's "Create your own burgers," Wednesday's grouper night, and Tuesday's all night early-bird special; excellent food in a fun, lively atmosphere; unexpected selection of international fare. ⑤ *Average main: $30* ✉ *Alhambra Mall, J. E. Irausquin Blvd. 47, Eagle Beach* ☎ *297/280–2518* ⊕ *www.twistofflavorsaruba.weebly.com.*

★ Windows on Aruba

$$$$ | **INTERNATIONAL** | This stylish, modern restaurant overlooking Divi Golf Village has become the reigning queen of Sunday feasting since they've dedicated themselves to serving only Royal Brunch. The comprehensive all-you-can-eat event includes endless mimosas, and gourmet surprises like Miso Sea Bass, Grilled Lamb Lollipops, and even Lobster Thermidor as mains, dozens of enticing appetizers and sides, and lots of decadent desserts. **Known for:** beautiful panoramic views from floor-to-ceiling windows; upscale gourmet fare; cosmopolitan bar area and stellar service. ⑤ *Average main: $55* ✉ *Divi Village Golf Resort, J. E. Irausquin Blvd. 41, Druif* ☎ *297/523–5017* ⊕ *www.windowsonaruba.com* ☽ *No dinner.*

☕ Coffee and Quick Bites

★ Beach Bar

$$ | **INTERNATIONAL** | Located across the street from Divi Village Golf & Beach Resort, this trendy beachfront spot serves the perfect seaside casual fare—panini, wraps, burgers, and salads—as well as great cocktails and often live entertainment. Enjoy superb sunset views there, and they also serve breakfast. **Known for:** great tapas and colorful creative cocktails; excellent burgers including vegan options; excellent service. ⑤ *Average main: $15* ✉ *Druif Beach, J.E. Irausquin Blvd. 41, Druif* ☎ *297/583–5000* ⊕ *www.facebook.com/BeachBarAruba.*

Pizza Bob's Restaurant & Pub

$$ | INTERNATIONAL | FAMILY | Grab a slice, a whole pizza to go, or a cold beer and snack at this friendly alfresco hideaway beside the Alhambra Mall. There are also pasta dishes, salads, wraps, BBQ options on the menu, as well as daily specials. **Known for:** Aruban-style pumpkin soup; great fried calamari; create-your-own pizza specials. ⑤ *Average main: $15* ⊠ *J. E. Irausquin Blvd. 57, Eagle Beach* ☎ *297/588–9040* ⊕ *pizzabobsaua.weebly.com.*

Santos Coffee with Soul

$ | INTERNATIONAL | Behind the Alhambra Mall, this is an ideal spot to get your gourmet coffee fix and grab some breakfast sandwiches to go before a beach day. Or stop and chat with locals at lunch enjoying barista-style coffees, gourmet sandwiches, and decadent desserts. **Known for:** friendly gathering spot; healthy smoothies and power breakfasts; special drinks of the month like "Dulce de leche latte". ⑤ *Average main: $10* ⊠ *Casa del Mar (in front of parking lot), J. E. Irausquin Blvd. 51, Eagle Beach* ☎ *297/280–0303* ⊕ *www.santos-aruba.com.*

 Hotels

The majority of hotels and resorts in this region were built to sprawl rather than tower, which is one reason why they call it the low-rise region. Most properties are no more than four stories tall, with Blue Residences as the exception. The Divi Resort family dominates the Druif Beach area with a collection of all-inclusives around their golf course.

Amsterdam Manor Beach Resort

$$ | HOTEL | FAMILY | Now with the distinction of being Aruba's only pet-friendly AAA Three Diamond hotel, Amsterdam Manor was first built in 1989 as a no-frills escape to attract Dutch visitors, especially families, seeking great value just steps from famed Eagle Beach. **Pros:** bright, clean, and eco-friendly oasis; home to famous romantic restaurant Passions on the Beach; warm family-run atmosphere with superb staff and service. **Cons:** small pool; not right on the beach; WaveRunners at beach can be noisy. ⑤ *Rooms from: $300* ⊠ *Eagle Beach, J. E. Irausquin Blvd. 252, Eagle Beach* ☎ *297/527–1100, 800/969–2310* ⊕ *www.amsterdam-manor.com* ⌖ *72 rooms* ⑨ *No Meals* ⌖ *Cashless resort.*

Aruba Beach Club

$ | TIMESHARE | FAMILY | One of the island's original time-share resorts was beginning to show its age, but 2021 saw all the rooms and suites undergo a major refresh and renovation and many of the common areas were nicely updated as well. **Pros:**

Amsterdam Manor Beach Resort, a small hotel on Eagle Beach, is still family-run.

good value; family-friendly atmosphere with kiddie pool and playground; soft white-sand beach. **Cons:** wave conditions can be dangerous for small children and poor swimmers; pool area can be very noisy; service can be lacking. $ *Rooms from: $225* ✉ *Punta Brabo Beach, J. E. Irausquin Blvd. 51–53, Punta Brabo* ☎ *297/524–3000* ⊕ *www.arubabeachclub.net* ➩ *131 rooms* ⦿ *No Meals.*

Blue Residences

$$$ | HOTEL | Bookended by Aruba's two most famous beaches (Eagle and Palm) on its own private man-made sandy strand right across the street, the Blue Residence Towers—one of three columns of condo hotel-style suites ranging from one to five bedrooms—offer epic unfettered views of the sea. **Pros:** lovely infinity pool looks out on the sea; full concierge services; all rooms have great sea views. **Cons:** far walk to shopping; not directly on the beach; little on-site entertainment. $ *Rooms from: $350* ✉ *J. E. Irausquin Blvd. 26, Eagle Beach* ☎ *297/525–3600* ⊕ *www.bluearuba.com* ➩ *120 rooms* ⦿ *No Meals* ☞ *There's a 3-night minimum.*

Bubali Bliss Studios

$ | HOTEL | Secreted behind Super Food, this economical and chic option is within walking distance of famed Eagle Beach, with beautifully decorated rooms (all of which have modern kitchens) and an inviting oasis pool surrounded by studios, deluxe studios, and one-bedroom apartments that are ideal for extended stays and workcations. **Pros:** free Wi-Fi; flexible anytime self-check-in and check-out; pool garden area with hammocks. **Cons:**

The beachfront at Bucuti & Tara Beach Resorts

three-night minimum stay requirement; not on a beach; no on-site dining. ⑤ *Rooms from: $200* ✉ *Bubali 147, behind Super Food, Eagle Beach* ☎ *297/587–5262* ⊕ *www.bubalibliss.com* ⤳ *10 rooms* ⑩ *No Meals* ⌇ *There's a 3-night minimum.*

★ Bucuti & Tara Beach Resort

$$$$ | HOTEL | Having achieved the first carbon-neutral status in the Caribbean, and winning multiple prestigious global eco awards, this landmark adults-only luxury boutique hotel offers exquisite personal service in an extraordinary beach setting. **Pros:** accessible management, with owners often on property; eco-friendly barefoot luxury at its best; unique arrival experience with personal concierge and iPad check-in. **Cons:** not all rooms have sea views; a little too quiet for some (no nighttime entertainment). ⑤ *Rooms from: $585* ✉ *L. G. Smith Blvd. 55B, Druif* ☎ *297/583–1100* ⊕ *www.bucuti.com* ⤳ *104 rooms* ⑩ *Free Breakfast.*

Casa del Mar Beach Resort

$ | RESORT | FAMILY | The one- and two-bedroom suites at this beachside time-share resort are quite comfortable though not overly luxe, and they come with fully equipped kitchens, and the resort offers a wide range of amenities like tennis courts and a gym and services like water sports and a kids' program. **Pros:** home-away-from-home feeling; family-friendly; popular Matthew's Beachside Restaurant is on-site. **Cons:** rooms feel a bit dated; charge for Wi-Fi; currents right offshore can be too strong for children. ⑤ *Rooms from: $225* ✉ *L. G. Smith Blvd. 53, Manchebo*

Beach ☎ *297/582–7000* ⊕ *www.casadelmar-aruba.com* ⇆ *147 rooms* ⦿ *No Meals.*

Costa Linda Beach Resort

$$$$ | **RESORT** | **FAMILY** | Operating like a small village unto itself, this all-suites, four-story, horseshoe-shaped time-share resort provides an ideal environment for families, with a kids' pool and colorful beachfront playground. **Pros:** great beach; spacious fully equipped suites; many activities available on-site. **Cons:** can get noisy when kids are everywhere; not all rooms have sea views; some rooms are outdated and there is no nightlife. ⑤ *Rooms from: $530* ⊠ *J. E. Irausquin Blvd. 59, Eagle Beach* ☎ *297/583–8000* ⊕ *www. costalinda-aruba.com* ⇆ *155 rooms* ⦿ *No Meals.*

★ Divi Aruba All-Inclusive

$$$$ | **RESORT** | The more upscale choice of Divi's sister all-inclusives, this resort is favored more by couples and honeymooners as the newer 60-room tower with its own pool and bar offers up some excellent sea views; there are four super-luxe two-bedroom oceanfront suites with whirlpool tubs. **Pros:** cosmopolitan lively vibe; on wonderful stretch of beach; eclectic choice of dining and entertainment. **Cons:** not all rooms have sea views; some older rooms are small by modern standards; reservations mandatory for the more upscale restaurants. ⑤ *Rooms from: $640* ⊠ *L. G. Smith Blvd. 93, Druif* ☎ *297/525–5200, 800/554–2008* ⊕ *www. diviaruba.com* ⇆ *269 rooms* ⦿ *All-Inclusive* ⌑ *There's a 3- or 5-night minimum.*

Divi Dutch Village Beach Resort

$$$ | **HOTEL** | **FAMILY** | This modern all-suites resort features very spacious, fully equipped accommodations ideal for families and small groups wishing to self cater; there's also an all-inclusive option that gives access to all the food and drink at both Divi Aruba and the Tamarijn. **Pros:** supermarkets are within walking distance; family-friendly wading pools; spacious suites fully equipped with modern appliances. **Cons:** no ocean views from most rooms; not directly on the beach; no nightly entertainment unless you go to sister resorts. ⑤ *Rooms from: $465* ⊠ *J. E. Irausquin Blvd. 47, Druif* ☎ *297/583–5000, 800/367–3484* ⊕ *www.dividutchvillage. com* ⇆ *123 rooms* ⦿ *No Meals* ⌑ *The all-inclusive options has a 3-night minimum.*

Divi Village Golf & Beach Resort

$$$ | **RESORT** | **FAMILY** | All the rooms at this all-suites golf resort community across the street from Druif Beach include fully equipped kitchens, but an all-inclusive option is also available with access and shuttles to sister resorts Tamarijn and Divi Aruba. **Pros:** lush and lovely grounds with freshwater lagoons and wildlife;

excellent golf course; dedicated beach space with lounge chairs and shade palapas across the street. **Cons:** the resort is not beach-front; no suites have two beds, only one bed and a sleeper sofa; no ocean-view rooms. $ *Rooms from: $455* ✉ *J. E. Irausquin Blvd. 93, Druif* ☎ *297/583–5000* ⊕ *www.divivillage.com* ⇋ *348 rooms* ⦿ *All-Inclusive* ☞ *The all-Inclusive option has a 3-night minimum.*

La Cabana Beach Resort & Casino
$$ | RESORT | FAMILY | A warm and friendly complex of mostly time-share units draws repeat visitors (primarily families) who enjoy the spacious accommodations equipped with everything you could possibly need for a home base away from home, including a fully equipped kitchen. **Pros:** lively family-friendly atmosphere with large pool facilities; laundry facilities on every floor; the only on-resort chapel on the island. **Cons:** few rooms have sea views; limited number of shade palapas; you must cross the road to get to the beach. $ *Rooms from: $300* ✉ *J. E. Irausquin Blvd. 250, Eagle Beach* ☎ *297/520–1100* ⊕ *www.lacabana.com* ⇋ *449 rooms* ⦿ *No Meals.*

Manchebo Beach Resort & Spa
$$ | RESORT | One of the original landmark low-rise resorts built on Aruba has refreshed and reinvented itself over the past few years to become a dedicated health and wellness resort with daily complimentary seafront yoga, Pilates classes, and healthy and healing cuisine menus. **Pros:** great on-site restaurants and culinary events; on the island's broadest and most pristine white-sand beach; all-inclusive meal plans available. **Cons:** not much in way of entertainment; rooms are on the small side; not all rooms have sea views. $ *Rooms from: $495* ✉ *J. E. Irausquin Blvd. 55, Man-chebo Beach* ☎ *297/522–3444, 800/223–1108* ⊕ *www.manchebo. com* ⇋ *72 rooms* ⦿ *Free Breakfast.*

★ Tamarijn Aruba All-Inclusive Beach Resort
$$$$ | RESORT | FAMILY | Having just received a major multimillion-dol-lar refreshment, the interiors of this popular all-inclusive now almost rival the stellar sea scenes mere steps from each door and the rooms (all oceanfront) have been outfitted with new technolo-gy and modern amenities like Nespresso machines and Smart TVs; king rooms also have sofa beds. **Pros:** complimentary Sea Turtle's Kids Club; children 12 and under stay and eat free; complimentary shuttle service between Divi resorts and the Alhambra Casino and Mall. **Cons:** no room service; beach entrance to sea can be rocky (beach shoes recommended); main pool can become crowded. $ *Rooms from: $640* ✉ *J. E. Irausquin Blvd. 41, Punta Brabo* ☎ *297/594–7888, 800/554–2008* ⊕ *www.tamarijnaruba.com* ⇋ *236 rooms* ⦿ *All-Inclusive* ☞ *There's a 3-night minimum.*

🍸 Nightlife

Most of the nightlife in this area revolves around the resorts where there are often special shows and live music for guests around pool areas, and some of their beach bars have regular special events like karaoke nights (the public is usually welcome).

BARS

Coco Loco Beach Bar and Restaurant

BARS | Just past Costa Linda Resort traveling toward the high-rise area, keep your eyes peeled for this colorful stand-alone beach shack that pops up out of nowhere on Eagle Beach; if you see a life-sized Captain Morgan outside, you'll know you're in the right spot! It's the quintessential colorful Caribbean-style beach bar by day, offering up snacks and tropical drinks, even shaved ice and fresh coconut water, but as the sun begins to set it often comes to life as a hot party spot luring folks to come dance barefoot in the sand to DJ-driven or live music. Beach lounges and umbrellas are available during the day if you want to take advantage of that prime Eagle Beach real estate while you indulge. ✉ *J.E. Irausquin Blvd. # 67A, Eagle Beach* ☎ *297/280–8081* ⊕ *www.facebook.com/ cocolocobeachbar.*

🛍 Shopping

This region isn't known for great shopping, though all the resorts have their own little stores and the area has the island's largest supermarkets—good to know if you're self-catering.

MALLS AND MARKETPLACES

★ The Shops at Alhambra Mall

SHOPPING CENTER | There's an eclectic array of shops and dining in alfresco Alhambra Mall with the casino as its focal point. Dotted with small retail stores and souvenir shops and a full-service market and deli, the mall also has multiple fast-food outlets as well as finer dining options like Fusions Wine & Tapas Bar, The Brownstone, and Twist of Flavors. There's often live music at night, and there's a small spa. Stores are open late, but the casino is open until the wee hours. ✉ *L. G. Smith Blvd. 47, Druif* ⊕ *www. facebook.com/alhambrashops.*

★ Super Food Plaza

SHOPPING CENTER | This massive complex offers all kinds of extras; it's more like a small department store. Beyond a huge fresh produce section, fresh fish and seafood market, bakery, and deli section, there's also a café, a drugstore, and even a toy store on-site. It's truly a one-stop for all your needs. ◼ TIP→ **Even if you**

are only on island for a week, chances are good you will make more than one visit here, so first trip, stop by the customer service desk and ask for a Tourist Bonus Card to save on all kinds of products and take advantage of weekly specials. They also deliver, and you can shop online and order curbside pick-up, too. ⊠ *Bubali 141-A, Eagle Beach* ☎ *297/522–2000* ⊕ *www.superfoodaruba.com.*

SPAS

★ Indulgence by the Sea Spa

SPAS | The spa-salon serving Divi Aruba and Tamarijn all-inclusives offers a wide range of premium services, but it's split into two locations. The salon that offers professional hair and nail care is located at Tamarijn Resort in a beautifully renovated glassed-in venue; it's very popular for specialty makeup and wedding hair. The spa portion is at Divi Aruba offering a full menu of facials, massages, and luxurious body treatments. All products are handpicked and tested by the owner Angie Wallace, who also owns Pure Indulgence Spa at the Divi Phoenix Resort. All of her spas are open to the public, and very popular with locals. ⊠ *J. E. Irausquin Blvd. 45, Druif* ☎ *297/583–0083 (Divi), 297/525–5291 (Tamarijn)* ⊕ *spaaruba.com.*

Purun Spa

SPAS | Reflecting the kind of upscale elegance and high-quality services one would expect of a spa located in adults-only luxury boutique Bucuti & Tara Beach Resort, this oasis of pampering offers a wide range of unique treatments with a focus on natural products and holistic health and wellness. There's even an outdoor cabana for massages and services. It's open to the public, but reservation preferences are given to resort guests. ⊠ *Bucuti & Tara Beach Resort, L. G. Smith Blvd. 55B, Eagle Beach* ☎ *297/583–1100* ⊕ *www.bucuti.com/wellness/spa.*

Spa del Sol

SPAS | An ideal Zen sanctuary right on the sea—and a partner to Manchebo resort's extensive health, wellness, and yoga services and retreats—this Balinese-themed spa hosts a bevy of partly open-air treatment rooms so you can hear the relaxing sounds of the waves; they even have hot tubs on the beach. A full range of treatments is available, including couple's massages. ⊠ *Manchebo Beach Resort, J. E. Irausquin Blvd. 55, Manchebo Beach* ☎ *297/582–6145* ⊕ *www.spadelsol.com.*

PALM BEACH AND NOORD AND WESTERN TIP (CALIFORNIA DUNES)

Updated by
Susan Campbell

5

◉ Sights	🍴 Restaurants	🛏 Hotels	🛍 Shopping	🍸 Nightlife
★★★★☆	★★★★☆	★★★★☆	★★★★☆	★★★★☆

NEIGHBORHOOD SNAPSHOT

TOP EXPERIENCES

■ **Swim, Stroll, People-Watch:** The island's liveliest stretch of sand and sea is unfettered by barriers or barricades.

■ **Water Sports Galore:** There's a wide assortment of water sports available along Palm Beach.

■ **Electric Tropical Nights:** The "strip" is full of bars, restaurants, cafés, and shops.

■ **Go Casino-Hopping:** Most high-rise hotels have their own glitzy casino, so you can hop from one to another without a car.

■ **Visit the Western Tip:** Climb the historic California lighthouse and explore the cool sand dunes surrounding it.

GETTING HERE AND AROUND

Palm Beach, part of the larger Noord region, is the island's liveliest tourism area and home to all the high-rise hotels.

Depending on traffic, it's about 25 minutes from the airport to the Palm Beach/Noord area; there's no public bus service directly from the airport. There's plenty of free parking around the high-rise hotels and beach area, as well as paid lots. Public buses from the Arubus terminal in Oranjestad stop at every major resort. Shared transport vans and private transfer options are available, as are taxis.

The new Watty Vos Blvd. (completed in 2019) provides a direct route from the airport to Palm Beach. If you're driving, be aware that there are a lot of round-abouts to navigate.

VIEWFINDER

■ This region has plenty of paradisia-cal beach scenes to capture, including the California Lighthouse—try it at sunrise instead of sunset for a whole different vibe—and the pan-oramic views from Alto Vista Chapel. There are also a few "I Love Aruba" type signs lit up at night along the Palm Beach strip for fun souvenir pics, but if you're seeking something more Insta-worthy, Paseo Herencia has an ethereal angel wings wall where you can pose for a unique pic.

NOORD

■ Once away from the hotels, Noord is all local neighbor-hoods with scenic little beach coves and sand dunes skirting the coast, culminating at the famous California Lighthouse.

Soft white sand for miles, clear aqua surf, lively beach bars, exciting water sports, fine dining, world-class casinos, superb shopping, electric nightlife, first-rate resorts—it's all within a stone's throw in Palm Beach. So park your car and get ready to pleasure-hop your way through Aruba's liveliest beach region, no matter the time of day.

Palm Beach and Noord

The district of Noord is home to the bulk of high-rise hotels and casinos that line Palm Beach. The hotels and restaurants, ranging from haute cuisine to fast food, are densely packed into a few miles running along the beachfront, while the bulk of the nightlife takes place across the street for about two miles down across the street from the hotels along J.E. Irausquin Boulevard, also known as "the strip." When other areas of Aruba are shutting down for the night, this area is guaranteed to still be buzzing with activity. Don't be afraid to venture outside of the tourism epicenter, though, because pristine wild coastal scenes and charming local neighborhoods await.

◉ Sights

Bubali Bird Sanctuary
NATURE PRESERVE | More than 80 species of migratory birds nest in this man-made wetland area inland from the island's strip of high-rise hotels. Herons, egrets, cormorants, coots, gulls, skimmers, terns, and ducks are among the winged wonders in and around the two interconnected artificial lakes that make up the sanctuary. Perch up on the wooden observation tower for great photo ops. (Bring bug repellent as the area is marshy and attracts mosquitoes.) ■TIP→ **Go early in the morning to see the most avian activity.** ✉ J. E. Irausquin Blvd., Noord ⊕ www.aruba.com/us/explore/bubali-bird-sanctuary ⛨ Free.

KEY

- ① Exploring Sights
- ① Restaurants
- ① Quick Bites
- ① Hotels

Druif Bay

Eagle Beach

J.E. Irausquin Blvd.

*Manchebo
Beach*

Divi
Village

0		1/2 mi
0		1/2 km

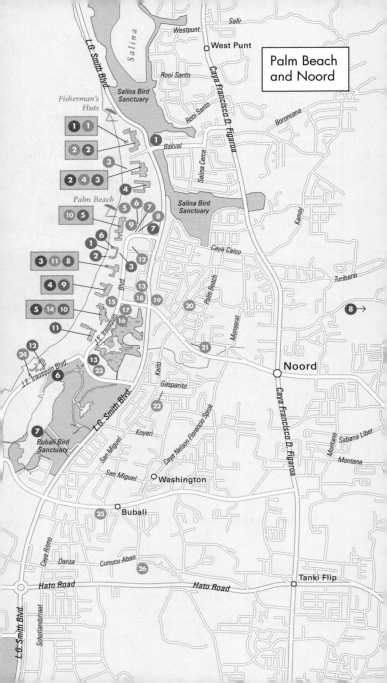

Palm Beach and Noord

★ Butterfly Farm

FARM/RANCH | **FAMILY** | Hundreds of butterflies and moths from around the world flutter about this spectacular garden. Guided tours (included in the price of admission) provide an entertaining look into the life cycle of these insects, from egg to caterpillar to chrysalis to butterfly or moth. After your initial visit, you can return as often as you like for free during your vacation. ■ TIP➔ **Go early in the morning when the butterflies are most active; wear bright colors if you want them to land on you.** Early morning is also when you are most likely to see the caterpillars emerge from their cocoons and transform into butterflies or moths. Their little Nectar Café out front serves refreshing drinks and homemade popsicles. ⊠ *J. E. Irausquin Blvd., across from Divi Phoenix Aruba Beach Resort, Palm Beach* ☎ *297/586–3656* ⊕ *www.thebutterflyfarm.com* ✉ *$16 (good for return visits).*

★ Philip's Animal Garden

FARM/RANCH | **FAMILY** | This nonprofit exotic animal rescue and reha-bilitation foundation is a wonderful, child-friendly attraction you'll find just off the beaten track up in Noord. Each guest is given a bag of treats for the animal residents, which include monkeys, peacocks, an emu, an ocelot, an alpaca, and many other types of creatures you're not likely to see elsewhere on Aruba. There's a large playground and ranch so little ones can run. It is also a stop on some tours. ⊠ *Alto Vista 116, Noord* ☎ *297/593–5363* ⊕ *www. philipsanimalgarden.com* ✉ *$10.*

CASINOS

The Casino Aruba

CASINO | This modern Vegas-style casino offers all the latest gaming options, upgraded machines, and lots of betting action like blackjack, poker, and roulette. Every day there is a different promotion or special for their VIP Players Club members (free of charge to join) and frequent poker tournaments. ⊠ *J. E. Irausquin Blvd. 81, Palm Beach* ☎ *297/526–6930* ⊕ *www.tcaruba.com* ☞ *No smoking allowed inside.*

★ The Casino at the Ritz-Carlton Aruba

CASINO | A very "ritzy" casino just off the lobby of the Ritz-Carlton Aruba offers many traditional table games like blackjack, craps, roulette, Caribbean stud poker, baccarat, and Texas hold 'em and more than 300 snazzy modern slots: spinning reels, video reels, and video games with jackpots. They also have two sports-betting kiosks and offer "luxury" bingo several times a week. Points accu-mulated from their VIP casino club card can be used toward hotel extras like dining, spa treatments, and room nights. ⊠ *L. G. Smith Blvd. 107, Palm Beach* ☎ *297/527–2222* ⊕ *www.ritzcarlton.com.*

Good-Luck Charms

Arubans take myths and superstitions very seriously. They flinch if a black butterfly flits into their home because this symbolizes death. And on New Year's Eve they toss the first sips of whiskey, rum, or champagne from the first bottle that's opened in the New Year out the door of their house to show respect to those who have died and to wish luck on others. It's no surprise, then, that good-luck charms are part of Aruba's casino culture as well.

The island's most common good-luck charm is the *djucu* (pronounced *joo-koo*), a brown-and-black nut that comes from the sea (usually from Venezuela) and becomes hot when rubbed. It's often called the "lucky nut" or "lucky stone." Many people have them put in gold settings— with their initials engraved in the metal—and wear them around their necks on a chain with other charms such as an anchor or a cross. Look for crafts and jewelry made from them in local artisan markets and at Cosecha.

Hyatt Regency Casino

CASINO | One of the island's smaller gaming spots, but just as glitzy, this recently enhanced casino offers 13 gaming tables, 148 slot machines, and 13 video poker machines. ⊠ *Hyatt Regency Aruba Beach Resort & Casino, J. E. Irausquin Blvd. 85, Palm Beach* ☎ *297/586–1234* ⊕ *www.hyatt.com.*

Liv Casino

CASINO | A small but welcoming little casino is just off the lobby of Barcelo Aruba Resort. It's a great spot to try your luck at some of the most modern slot games. They also have blackjack and roulette and there are also some interesting promotions every week. ⊠ *Barcelo Aruba Resort, J. E. Irausquin Blvd. 82, Palm Beach* ☎ *297/280–4000* ⊕ *www.liv-casino.com.*

★ Stellaris Casino

CASINO | This is one of the largest casinos on the island. There are 500 modern interactive slots as well as 26 tables with games like craps, roulette, poker, and blackjack. There's a state-of-the-art race and sports-betting operation. Don't forget to join the VIP Club program, where you can earn points, comps, and prizes. They offer free cocktails for gamers, and there are many special theme and entertainment nights. ⊠ *Aruba Marriott Resort, L. G. Smith Blvd. 101, Palm Beach* ☎ *297/586–9000* ⊕ *www.stellariscasino.com.*

Beaches

Fisherman's Huts (*Hadicurari*)

BEACH | Beside the Ritz-Carlton, Fisherman's Huts is a windsurf-er's, kiteboarder's, and now "wing-foiling" haven. Swimmers might have a hard time avoiding all the boards going by; as this is the nexus of where the lessons take place for these water sports, it's always awash in students and experts and board hobbyists. It's a gorgeous spot to just sit and watch the sails on the sea, and lately, it's become increasingly popular among paddleboarders and sea kayakers, too. Only drinks and small snacks are available at the operator's shacks. There are no restrooms, but the Ritz lobby is nearby in a pinch. **Amenities:** food and drink; parking (free); water sports. **Best for:** windsurfing. ⊠ *Palm Beach* ⊹ *North of Aruba Marriott Resort.*

★ Palm Beach

BEACH | This is the island's most populated and popular beach running along the high-rise resorts, and it's crammed with every kind of water-sports activity and food-and-drink emporium imagi-nable. It's always crowded no matter the season, but it's a great place for people-watching, sunbathing, swimming, and partying; and there are always activities happening like paddleboarding, and even paddleboard yoga. The water is pond-calm; the sand, pow-der-fine. **Amenities:** food and drink; showers; toilets; water sports. **Best for:** partiers; swimming. ⊠ *J. E. Irausquin Blvd. between Divi Phoenix Resort and Ritz-Carlton Aruba, Palm Beach.*

 Restaurants

Aqua Grill

$$$$ | **SEAFOOD** | Aficionados flock here to enjoy a wide selection of seafood and fish in a New England–style decor. Dishes like smoked swordfish and grilled red snapper served with a mango salsa are top of the list, and they also nod to a New England feel with Maine lobster. **Known for:** consistently high-quality specials; daily fresh seafood, either from local fishermen or flown in; massive raw bar. ⑤ *Average main: $35* ⊠ *J. E. Irausquin Blvd. 374, Palm Beach* ☎ *297/586–5900* ⊕ *www.aqua-grill.com.*

Atardi

$$$$ | **INTERNATIONAL** | This rollicking beach bar by day morphs into a surprisingly romantic pop-up, toes-in-the-sand dining spot as soon as the sun begins to set—the sunsets rarely disappoint. Fresh fish and seafood are the specialty but meat lovers will be

well sated with the excellent filet mignon and short ribs dishes.
Known for: excellent fish and seafood; torchlit, seaside dining;
attentive personal service. Ⓢ *Average main: $45* ✉ *Aruba Marriott
Resort, L. G. Smith Blvd. 101, Palm Beach* ☎ *297/520–6537*
⊕ *www.marriott.com.*

★ Azia Restaurant Lounge

$$$ | ASIAN FUSION | Secreted away just off the main Palm Beach
strip, seek out the hidden Buddha to find the twinkling lights that
lead to an absolutely enchanting upscale Asian-fusion emporium
with stunning decor and Aruba's longest bar. Enjoy an eclectic
selection of dim sum, sushi, and creative meat and seafood dishes that can be paired with sake, Japanese beer, and whiskey, or a
killer handcrafted cocktail from their expert mixologists. **Known for:**
excellent sushi; great for groups as it seats 350 and has excellent shareables; semiprivate room for up to 12 people is unique
to the island. Ⓢ *Average main: $30* ✉ *J. E. Irausquin Blvd. 348,
Palm Beach* ✛ *Across the street from the Hilton* ☎ *297/586–0088*
⊕ *www.aziaaruba.com.*

Bavaria Food & Beer

$$$ | GERMAN | A variety of German beers, schnitzel, and bratwurst
presented in a true beer-hall setting are guaranteed to provide that
Oktoberfest feeling. The hearty cuisine is paired with over 20 different types of beer by owners who take their imbibing seriously.
Known for: outdoor beer garden suitable for large groups; German
cuisine served in an "oom-pa-pa" atmosphere; fun and friendly
crowd of locals and visitors. Ⓢ *Average main: $25* ✉ *Palm Beach
186, Noord* ☎ *297/586–8550* ⊕ *www.bavaria-aruba.com* ☽ *Closed
Sun.*

BLT Steak

$$$$ | AMERICAN | Though this restaurant in the Ritz-Carlton is
designed to replicate a New York–style steak house, if you're
looking for a more Caribbean feel, opt for the ethereal dining
room that leads out to a breezy garden terrace just steps from
the sea for stellar sunset views that are unmistakably Caribbean.
And though it's supposed to be all about the meat here, their
very pricey but comprehensive seafood platter called *The Royale*
is worth the splurge. **Known for:** surprising selection of East and
West coast oysters; 28-day, dry-aged porterhouse for two; USDA
Prime 100% naturally raised certified Black Angus beef. Ⓢ *Average main: $60* ✉ *Ritz-Carlton Aruba, L. G. Smith Blvd. 107, Palm
Beach* ☎ *297/527–2399* ⊕ *www.bltrestaurants.com.*

Bohemian

$$$$ | INTERNATIONAL | Secreted away near the Barcelo resort you'll find a hip, little laid-back tropical oasis of tiki-style huts and "bohemian" escapes with a focus on French and world cuisine, sometimes with a local Caribbean twist. It's well worth seeking out for the cool vibe and eclectic choice of fare ranging from raclette or ginger and honey duck to braised lamb or paella, with some creative vegetarian and vegan options thrown in. **Known for:** comprehensive European wine list; fresh mussels flown in from Holland when available; homemade fois gras and excellent charcuterie and cheese plates. $ *Average main: $40 ⊠ JE Irausquin Blvd. 83, Beside the Barcelo, Palm Beach* ☎ *297/280–8448* ⊕ *bohemianaruba.com* ⊗ *No lunch.*

★ Casa Nonna

$$$$ | ITALIAN | The cheery Ritz-Carlton breakfast spot known as Solanio takes on a whole new identity in the evenings as it transforms into Casa Nonna (meaning grandmother's house), dedicated to serving up authentic Italian cuisine. Service is exquisite (they even have a cocktail cart) and you can taste the care put into the handmade pastas and sauces. **Known for:** top-quality cured meats and cheeses; authentic house-made pastas and sauces; Mediterranean comfort food, sometimes with a fusion twist. $ *Average main: $40 ⊠ Ritz-Carlton Aruba, L. G. Smith Blvd. 107, Noord* ☎ *297/527–2222* ⊕ *www.casanonna.com* ⊗ *Closed Tues.*

★ Da Vinci Ristorante

$$$$ | ITALIAN | FAMILY | Don't let the rustic decor fool you: this is not your average Italian resort eatery, though it's an inviting choice for large groups. Da Vinci pulls out all the stops to present a seriously upscale, authentic, and creative menu of Mediterranean favorites. **Known for:** family-friendly yet upscale atmosphere; creative Italian fare; excellent wine cellar. $ *Average main: $35 ⊠ Holiday Inn Resort Aruba, J. E. Irausquin Blvd. 230, Palm Beach* ☎ *297/586–3600* ⊕ *www.holidayarubaresort.com* ⊗ *Closed Sun.*

★ Fireson Brewing Company

$$ | INTERNATIONAL | If you're seeking something more pubby than clubby, sleuth out this casual and comforting spot tucked away on Cove Mall's far corner facing the Holiday Inn parking lot. It's all about the beer and the bites here, as Fireson offers up their own craft beer and authentic Aruban comfort food like funchi fries with cheese, croquettes, and empanadas (pastechis' close cousin). **Known for:** shareable plates for 4-6 people; excellent craft beer; comfort food pub fare. $ *Average main: $12 ⊠ J.E. Irausquin Blvd 230, Palm Beach* ☎ *297/561–6100* ⊕ *www.firesonbrewing.com* ⊗ *Closed Tues. No lunch.*

Gasparito Restaurant & Art Gallery

$$$ | CARIBBEAN | This enchanting hideaway can be found in a beautifully restored 200-year-old *cunucu* (country) house, where you can dine indoors or out. Aruban specialties including *keshi yena* and Gasparito chicken (with brandy, white wine, pineapple, and four secret ingredients) are on the menu, the latter with a sauce passed down through the owner's family. **Known for:** very limited seatings with required reservations; a unique country-house setting that is part art gallery; time-honored Aruban specialties. ⑤ *Average main: $30* ✉ *Gasparito 3, Noord* ☎ *297/594–2550* ⊕ *www.gasparito.com* ⊗ *Closed Sun.*

Hanaski Fusion

$$$ | FUSION | The gorgeously decorated emporium near the Old Windmill is awash in cherry blossoms and soft neon with ultra-modern accents and an exciting, inviting feel, but the biggest surprise is the fusion of cuisines all under the same little roof. The menu features a mix of elegantly presented Japanese and Peruvian fare with excellent sushi renditions as well. **Known for:** fresh preparations of ceviche and sushi; eclectic fusions of three different cuisines; special themed nights and all-night-long happy hour 2-for-1 specials. ⑤ *Average main: $25* ✉ *J.E. Irausquin Blvd. 330, next to Courtyard by Marriott, Palm Beach* ☎ *297/730–2244* ⊗ *No lunch.*

Hostaria Da' Vittorio

$$$ | ITALIAN | FAMILY | At one of Aruba's most celebrated Italian eateries, part of the fun at this family-oriented spot is watching chef Vittorio Muscariello prepare authentic Italian regional specialties in his open kitchen. The staff helps you choose wines from the extensive list and recommends portions of hot and cold antipasti, risottos, and pastas. **Known for:** good for large groups; brick-oven pizza; beautiful courtyard dining space. ⑤ *Average main: $30* ✉ *L. G. Smith Blvd. 380, Palm Beach* ☎ *297/586–3838* ⊕ *www. hostariavittorio.com.*

The Lazy Turtle

$$$ | INTERNATIONAL | This sprawling spot takes over an entire side of Paseo Herencia's interior courtyard, offering up an eclectic mix of dining and rollicking bar life. Interesting specialties like African smoked fish and *Kuvuta Kuku* (an African style of chicken) are served alongside pastas, steaks, and fresh fish and seafood. **Known for:** interesting menu choices; lively gathering spot; excellent bartender and fancy drinks. ⑤ *Average main: $25* ✉ *Paseo Herencia Mall, J.E. Irausquin Blvd. 382A, Palm Beach* ☎ *297/592–0369* ⊕ *thelazyturtlearuba.com* ⊗ *No lunch.*

Jumbo shrimp are a delicious staple at Madame Janette.

Madame Janette

$$$$ | **EUROPEAN** | The food at this rustic restaurant, named after the Scotch bonnet pepper called Madame Janette in Aruba, is surprisingly not Caribbean spicy, but French-inspired from the classically trained chef. Though many dishes are infused with Caribbean flavors, especially fish and seafood, you'll find a lot of classic sauces served with the meat; surprisingly, there are a number of specialty schnitzels on the menu. **Known for:** specials that focus on local seasonal ingredients; top-quality meat and seafood; craft beers and even a beer sommelier. $ *Average main: $40* ⌧ *Cunucu Abao 37, Cunucu Abao* ☎ *297/587–0184* ⊕ *www.madamejanette.info* ✆ *Closed Sun. No lunch.*

MooMba Beach Bar & Restaurant

$$$ | **INTERNATIONAL** | Best known as a beach party spot, this legendary hangout has good food and is a popular place for a seafront breakfast. Dinner under the giant shaded palapa is first-rate, as is lunch—particularly since it's the perfect place for people-watching along Aruba's busiest beach. **Known for:** 1-pound racks of honey-glazed ribs; daily all-you-can-eat prix-fixe breakfast buffet; variety of giant pinchos (skewered meats). $ *Average main: $30* ⌧ *J. E. Irausquin Blvd. 230, Palm Beach* ☎ *297/586–5365* ⊕ *www.moombabeach.com.*

Old Cunucu House

$$$ | **CARIBBEAN** | Since the mid-1990s executive chef Ligia Maria has delighted diners with delicious and authentic *crioyo* (local) cuisine in a rustic and cozy traditional cunucu house. Try the house version of Aruba's famous keshi yena—chicken, raisins, olives, cashews, peppers, and rice in a hollowed-out Gouda rind—or thick, hearty *stobas* (stews) of goat or beef. **Known for:** family-run and family-friendly atmosphere; secret family recipes of traditional Aruban cuisine; hearty portions and good prices. ⑤ *Average main: $25* ⊠ *Palm Beach 150, Palm Beach* ☎ *297/586–1666* ⊕ *www. theoldcunucuhouse.com.*

★ Papillon

$$$$ | **FRENCH** | The jailhouse theme may take you aback (it's inspired by the famous Devil's Island prisoner Henri Charrière), but the popular landmark spot on the strip will win you over with its delicious French-Caribbean fusion cuisine enjoyed in their massive courtyard. The menu includes classics like frogs' legs, escargots, caviar, and French onion soup as well as duck with passion-fruit sauce and local snapper with grilled shrimp and a creole sauce. **Known for:** bargain-priced, early-bird prix-fixe menu; prix-fixe six-course Chef's Garden Menu with wine pairing; classic French old-school cuisine with a slight Caribbean twist. ⑤ *Average main: $35* ⊠ *J. E. Irausquin Blvd. 348A, Palm Beach* ☎ *297/586–5400* ⊕ *www.papillonaruba.com.*

★ pureocean

$$$$ | **CONTEMPORARY** | Unfettered sea views and stellar sunsets with tiki lights and lit-up palms make this the signature dining spot of Divi Aruba Phoenix. The menu offers continental favorites with a Caribbean twist, and guests can enjoy fish, steak, and seafood beachside in the bistro or with toes in the sand mere steps from the sea. **Known for:** Wine Down Fridays (prix-fixe happy hour with wine and tapas); romantic seaside dinners; a wide selection of international fare. ⑤ *Average main: $35* ⊠ *Divi Aruba Phoenix Beach Resort, J. E. Irausquin Blvd. 75, Palm Beach* ☎ *297/586– 6066* ⊕ *www.pureoceanrestaurant.com.*

★ Quinta del Carmen

$$$$ | **DUTCH** | Set in a beautifully restored 100-year-old mansion with a lovely outdoor courtyard, Quinta del Carmen's cuisine is best defined as modern Caribbean-Dutch. There are a few traditional Dutch favorites like cheese croquettes and mushrooms and cream, and the watermelon salad is sweet, salty, and perfectly refreshing, while the *sucade-lappen* (flank steak stewed in red

wine and herbs) has a depth of flavor that comes from hours in the pot. **Known for:** gorgeous antique mansion setting full of avant-garde art; upscale Dutch comfort food; tapas garden for shareables. [$] *Average main: $40* ⊠ *Bubali 119, Noord* ☎ *297/587–7200* ⊕ *www.quintadelcarmen.com.*

Rotisserie la Braise

$$ | EUROPEAN | What started as a classic French restaurant has splintered into three distinct alfresco sections—French, Greek, and Italian—with separate menus and separate chefs, but still under the same roof. So whether you're in the mood for frog's legs, moussaka, or pasta, this is the spot, plus there are wines from all three regions, too. **Known for:** excellent French, Italian, and Greek cuisine; great Sunday brunch; rotisserie chicken to go. [$] *Average main: $20* ⊠ *Cove Mall, J.E. Irausquin Blvd. 384-A, Palm Beach* ☎ *297/280–0300* ⊕ *www.facebook.com/rotisseriela-braise* ☉ *No lunch.*

Ruinas del Mar

$$$$ | CARIBBEAN | This scenic spot is famous for its gorgeous circuit of waterfalls cascading around stone "ruins" that offers the ideal setting for romantic dinners and sunny breakfasts. Indoor dining affords a lagoon view while the outdoor terrace overlooks a koi pond. **Known for:** the resident black swans; romantic setting for date night; a comprehensive specialty coffee menu. [$] *Average main: $45* ⊠ *Hyatt Regency Aruba Beach Resort and Casino, J. E. Irausquin Blvd. 85, Palm Beach* ☎ *297/586–1234* ⊕ *aruba.hyatt.com* ☉ *No lunch.*

Ruth's Chris Steak House

$$$$ | AMERICAN | This American steak house chain has been a popular fixture of the Aruba Marriott for years and continues to draw locals and visitors in droves. It is a no-nonsense carnivore's delight with the focus on top-quality steak; those looking for something else will find a few interesting seafood specialties like Louisiana-style barbecue shrimp and sizzling blue crab cakes. **Known for:** Porterhouse for two; top-quality USDA prime beef; famous dipping trio for steaks: black truffle butter, shiitake demi-glace, and honey soy glaze. [$] *Average main: $50* ⊠ *Aruba Marriott Resort and Stellaris Casino, L. G. Smith Blvd. 103, Palm Beach* ☎ *297/520–6600* ⊕ *www.ruthschris.com* ☉ *No lunch.*

Sunset Grille

$$$$ | INTERNATIONAL | Simple and elegant, without a lot of extra gimmicks, this is a no-nonsense modern steak and seafood spot with a focus on fresh and locally sourced ingredients whenever possible. Though there's air-conditioned seating inside, grab a

seat outside for dinner to find out why this is called the Sunset Grille. **Known for:** Aruban seafood risotto; prix-fixe chef's collection dinner for two; sunset surf and turf. $ *Average main: $45* ⊠ *Hilton Aruba, J. E. Irausquin Blvd. 81, Noord* ☎ *297/586–6555* ⊕ *www. hiltonaruba.com.*

2 Fools and a Bull Gourmet Studio
$$$$ | **INTERNATIONAL** | One of Aruba's very first forays into the chef's table experience, here you'll enjoy an intimate evening of culinary entertainment that plays like a fun dinner party with friends rather than something you pay for. At most, 14 guests are assembled around the U-shaped communal dinner table for a five-and-a-half course creative gourmet adventure. **Known for:** adults-only with reservations required far in advance; an intimate chef's table experience; perfect wine pairings (optional). $ *Average main: $130* ⊠ *Palm Beach 17, Noord* ☎ *297/586–7177* ⊕ *www. 2foolsandabull.com* ☉ *Closed weekends.*

★ The Vue Rooftop Aruba
$$$ | **INTERNATIONAL** | The crowning glory of all the options at the new Cove Mall is this aptly named second-story bar and restaurant where a private elevator introduces guests to incredible vistas at any time of day. But it's not so much the view that draws the crowds here as it is the vibe—think private beach cabanas with killer mixologists behind the bar, and romantic tables for two scattered around a rooftop. **Known for:** exquisite hand-crafted cocktails; exclusive VIP cabana rentals with luxe amenties; trendy hot spot for the "beautiful people." $ *Average main: $30* ⊠ *The Cove Mall, J.E. Irausquin Blvd. 384-A, Palm Beach* ☎ *297/280–0279* ⊕ *www.thevuerooftoparuba.com* ☉ *No lunch Mon.–Sat.*

★ YOLO Cocktails & Tapas
$$ | **INTERNATIONAL** | If you only live once (YOLO), here's a place to cram as many cool experiences into your holiday as possible. Self-described as an entertainment and event venue, YOLO is really three hotspots and cool concepts in one—by day, it's a gourmet pancake factory, but at night it becomes a rollicking indoor/outdoor space with music, uber-creative tapas like *Crispy Pork Belly Jerk Mofongo,* and humongous craft cocktails for two–six people to share. **Known for:** Dutch, American, Belgian, and Japanese pancakes available; humongous craft cocktails that two–six people can share; three cool concepts in one. $ *Average main: $20* ⊠ *The Cove Mall, J.E. Irausquin Blvd 384-A, Palm Beach* ☎ *297/280–0029* ⊕ *yoloaruba.com.*

Coffee and Quick Bites

Dushi Bagels & Burgers

$ | **INTERNATIONAL** | Family-owned and run since 2008, this is the spot to come for the island's best assortment of bagels, as well as smoothies and shakes, bagel sandwiches, wraps, and gourmet burgers. The menu also includes great beach-side dining options like salads, fish and chips, and bar-food apps that pair well with the daily happy hour (i.e. mozzarella sticks and nachos). **Known for:** barista-style hot and iced coffees; vegan specialties also available; largest selection of bagels on Aruba. $ *Average main: $10* ⊠ *Playa Linda Beach Resort, Irausquin Blvd. 87, Palm Beach* ☎ *297/586–3035* ⊕ *dushibagelsandburgers.com.*

Eduardo's Beach Shack

$ | **INTERNATIONAL** | This cheery little hut on Palm Beach is famous for their healthy and delicious fresh fruit and veggie juices, smoothies, bowls, and creative vegan options. All of their specialties are free of additives and artificial substances. **Known for:** large selection of healthy bowls and smoothies; fresh, healthy and delicious fare; soft serve dairy-free ice cream. $ *Average main: $11* ⊠ *J. E. Irausquin Blvd. 87, In front of Playa Linda Resort, Noord* ☎ *297/699–9823* ⊕ *www.eduardosbeachshack.com.*

Scott's Brats

$ | **INTERNATIONAL** | The expat American owners brought a taste of home to their alfresco Palm Beach bar hut with authentic Wisconsin brats and sausages and Chicago-style hot dogs, and they have funnel cakes too. They also make some killer creative cocktails and serve coffee. **Known for:** "Funky Fries" menu with weird yet tasty toppings; sandwiches and rolls stuffed with meat; ribs, chicken, sausages, and tacos. $ *Average main: $10* ⊠ *J. E. Irausquin Blvd. 87, Palm Beach* ⊕ *scottsbratsaruba.weebly.com.*

Hotels

Aruba Marriott Resort & Stellaris Casino

$$$$ | **RESORT** | **FAMILY** | This full-service resort offers both family-friendly amenities as well as an adults-only luxury floor that has its own pool and snazzy lounge on the ground floor. **Pros:** one of the island's best casinos; lots of water sports options right out front; adults-only oasis and adults-only floor. **Cons:** not all rooms have sea views; main pool can be noisy and crowded with kids; beachfront can become crowded in high season. $ *Rooms from: $599* ⊠ *L. G. Smith Blvd. 101, Palm Beach* ☎ *297/586–9000, 800/223–6388* ⊕ *www.marriott.com* ⇴ *414 rooms* ⦿ *No Meals.*

Barcelo Aruba

$$$$ | RESORT | FAMILY | This family-friendly all-inclusive offers something for everyone, with an extensive pool complex, great nightly entertainment, a dedicated kids' club, and an eclectic choice of à la carte dining. **Pros:** excellent location for Palm Beach water sports and shopping; spacious rooms, many with good sea views; Royal Club level has a dedicated dining room and lounge. **Cons:** difficult to get a shaded beach lounge if you don't go early; beach in front can get very crowded; pool area can be very noisy with activities. $ *Rooms from: $770* ⊠ *J. E. Irausquin Blvd. 83, Palm Beach* 🕾 *297/586–4500* ⊕ *www.barcelo.com* 🍽 *All-Inclusive* ⇱ *373 rooms.*

★ Boardwalk Boutique Hotel Aruba

$$$ | HOTEL | What began as a tiny family-run boutique hotel has since evolved into an entire Caribbean cottage-style community of "casitas" connected by a signature wooden boardwalk. **Pros:** intimate small resort vibe with many secret oasis spots; stellar personal service and small village vibe; modern digital amenities like key and concierge apps and 5G Wi-Fi. **Cons:** no on-site entertainment; not right on the beach; smokers must indulge outside of the property's security gates. $ *Rooms from: $450* ⊠ *Bakval 20, Palm Beach* 🕾 *297/586–6654* ⊕ *www.boardwalkaruba.com* ⇱ *46 units* 🍽 *No Meals.*

Courtyard by Marriot Aruba Resort

$ | HOTEL | A bright, contemporary economical alternative to the high-rises on Palm Beach, this property is ideally suited for work-cations or small group getaways with modern rooms outfitted with the latest technology, and an inviting pool area that includes a swim-up bar. **Pros:** walking distance to the beach; clean modern rooms; great value. **Cons:** little entertainment; not right on the sea; beach chairs do not include shade palapas. $ *Rooms from: $250* ⊠ *J E Irausquin Blvd. 330, Palm Beach* 🕾 *297/586–7700* ⊕ *www. marriott.com* 🍽 *No Meals* ⇱ *192 rooms.*

★ Divi Aruba Phoenix Beach Resort

$$$$ | RESORT | FAMILY | With incredible views from its high-rise tower, stunning rooms awash in tropical colors and state-of-the-art amenities, and comfortable, homey accommodations, Divi Aruba Phoenix rises above the fray on busy Palm Beach. **Pros:** all units have sea views; beautifully appointed rooms, some with whirlpool bathtubs; great private beach away from the main Palm Beach frenzy. **Cons:** no all-inclusive plan; no shuttle service to other Divi properties; no reserving shade palapas. $ *Rooms from: $740* ⊠ *J. E. Irausquin Blvd. 75, Palm Beach* 🕾 *297/586–1170* ⊕ *www. diviarubaphoenix.com* ⇱ *240 rooms* 🍽 *No Meals.*

The Aruba Marriott Resort & Stellaris Casino is in the heart of Palm Beach.

Hilton Aruba Caribbean Resort and Casino

$$$$ | **HOTEL** | **FAMILY** | Sprawling over 15 acres of white sand and lush tropical gardens with a lovely water circuit winding through-out, this iconic resort is located where the first hotel to debut on Palm Beach in 1959 and was the birthplace of the famous Aruba Ariba cocktail. **Pros:** grand ballroom is ideal for big events; excel-lent beachfront area never feels crowded, even when at capacity; Palm Beach Club VIP program has special perks and a lounge. **Cons:** food and drink can be pricey; not all rooms have sea views; sometimes long lines at the breakfast buffets. ⑤ *Rooms from: $600* ✉ *J. E. Irausquin Blvd. 81, Palm Beach* ☎ *297/586–6555* ⊕ *www.hiltonaruba.com* ⑩ *No Meals* ⌇ *357 rooms.*

★ Holiday Inn Resort Aruba

$$$ | **RESORT** | **FAMILY** | The resort's massive lemon-yellow buildings that sprawl across a prime spot on Palm Beach offer a revelation compared to what most might think a Holiday Inn stay might entail—inviting rooms, a fun vibe, and distinct sections that will appeal to those looking for quiet active fun or a family-friend-ly environment. **Pros:** excellent on-site dining can include an all-inclusive meal plan; thematic zones provide distinct amenities; kids stay free and enjoy an excellent stand-alone kids' club. **Cons:** sometimes hard to get a palapa; not all rooms have sea views; reception is frequently busy with big groups. ⑤ *Rooms from: $415* ✉ *J. E. Irausquin Blvd. 230, Palm Beach* ☎ *297/586–3600,*

800/465–4329 ⊕ *www.holidayarubaresort.com* ✍ *590 rooms* ❢⊙❢ *No Meals.*

Hotel Riu Palace Aruba

$$$$ | **RESORT** | **FAMILY** | This family-friendly all-inclusive is a massive complex surrounding an expansive water circuit with a choice of five restaurants and scads of free activities. **Pros:** nice shallow beachfront; spacious water circuit for families; a wide choice of entertainment and dining. **Cons:** few spots to escape in solitude; beach and pool area get very busy and noisy; few rooms have unobstructed sea views. $ *Rooms from: $630* ⊠ *J. E. Irausquin Blvd. 79, Palm Beach* ☎ *297/586–3900* ⊕ *www.riu.com* ❢⊙❢ *All-Inclusive* ✍ *400 rooms.*

Hyatt Regency Aruba Resort Spa and Casino

$$$$ | **RESORT** | **FAMILY** | Located on 12 acres of prime beachfront, the rooms and suites at this landmark resort have all been recently refreshed and welcome couples as well as families. **Pros:** many rooms have spectacular ocean views; luxurious adults-only beachfront pool; lush tropical landscaping leads down to spacious beachfront. **Cons:** some standard rooms are on the small side with small balconies; few rooms have full balconies; not all rooms have sea views. $ *Rooms from: $599* ⊠ *J. E. Irausquin Blvd. 85, Palm Beach* ☎ *297/586–1234, 800/554–9288* ⊕ *www.hyatt.com* ❢⊙❢ *No Meals* ✍ *359 rooms.*

Marriott's Aruba Ocean Club

$$$$ | **TIMESHARE** | **FAMILY** | First-rate amenities and lavishly decorated villas with balconies and full kitchens have made this timeshare an island favorite. **Pros:** excellent beach; relaxed atmosphere; feels more like a home than a hotel room. **Cons:** attracts large families, so lots of kids are about; beach can get crowded; grounds are not in sea view. $ *Rooms from: $771* ⊠ *L. G. Smith Blvd. 99, Palm Beach* ☎ *297/586–2641* ⊕ *www.marriott.com* ✍ *218 rooms* ❢⊙❢ *No Meals.*

Playa Linda Beach Resort

$$$$ | **TIMESHARE** | **FAMILY** | Looking something like a stepped Mayan pyramid—the design maximizes sea views from the balconies—this older timeshare hotel also has a homey feel, with full kitchens in all the spacious units. **Pros:** lots of distractions for the kids; great beach location; spacious rooms and townhomes. **Cons:** can be a crowded and busy beachfront; not all rooms are of the same standard; not all rooms have sea views. $ *Rooms from: $577* ⊠ *J. E. Irausquin Blvd. 87, Palm Beach* ☎ *297/586–1000* ⊕ *www.playalinda.com* ❢⊙❢ *No Meals* ✍ *144 rooms, 3 townhomes.*

★ Radisson Blu Aruba

$$$ | HOTEL | FAMILY | The stylish new high-rise behind the Palm Beach strip towers to 14 floors that overlook a gorgeous water circuit. **Pros:** expansive water circuit includes an adults-only pool and a whirlpool nook; ideal for families that want to self cater; two floors of premium penthouse suites. **Cons:** not all rooms have balconies; not all rooms have sea views; not on the beach. ⑤ *Rooms from: $400* ⊠ *J.E. Irausquin Blvd. #97-A, Noord* ☎ *866/856–9066* ⊕ *www.radissonhotelsamericas.com* ❑ *No Meals* ⤳ *132 rooms.*

★ Ritz-Carlton, Aruba

$$$$ | HOTEL | This massive hotel sits on a broad stretch of white sand with all rooms overlooking the sea. **Pros:** exemplary personal service; spacious grounds so it never feels crowded; stunning sunset views from rooms and the atrium lobby bar. **Cons:** sheer size and design gives it a big-box feel; attracts many large groups; pricey compared to other similar properties. ⑤ *Rooms from: $750* ⊠ *L. G. Smith Blvd. 107, Palm Beach* ☎ *527–2222* ⊕ *www.ritzcarlton.com* ❑ *No Meals* ⤳ *320 rooms.*

Nightlife

The 2-mile stretch of road in front of the high-rise resorts called The Strip is where you'll find most of the nightlife action in Palm Beach, and the new Cove Mall has become an anchor of new hot spots. The clubs tend to come and go, but The Strip is always chock-full of opportunities to let loose after the sun goes down in the area's squares, courtyards, and outdoor malls, and threaded throughout are vendor kiosks. You can easily barhop or casinohop on foot to find the vibe that suits you best by following the music that moves you. If you're staying in a Palm Beach resort, there's no need for a car or taxi.

BARS

★ Bugaloe Bar & Grill

BARS | Night and day, this crazy colorful beach bar at the tip of De Palm Pier on busy Palm Beach is packed. Paint-spattered wooden tables and chairs on a plank floor under a massive palapa draw barefoot beachcombers in for frozen cocktails, cold beer, and casual fare where live music is king. There are karaoke nights, salsa nights, and daily food specials. It's also an optimal spot to catch a magical sunset over the waves. ⊠ *De Palm Pier, J. E. Irausquin Blvd. 79, Palm Beach* ☎ *297/586–2233* ⊕ *www.bugaloe.com.*

The Bulldog Aruba

BARS | Based on the famous Bulldog in the Netherlands, this one is all about partying hearty in the center of Paseo Herencia's

courtyard with zany antics by the barkeeps and lots of dance action after the water shows end. There are food and drink specials, but it's really all about drinking and dancing, karaoke nights, beer pong, creative cocktails, and techno music. ⊠ *Paseo Herencia Mall 382A, Palm Beach* ☎ *297/563–7951* ⊕ *www.facebook. com/thebulldogaruba.*

Craft & Lola

GATHERING PLACES | These odd combination sister spots are hard to miss on the Palm Beach strip with their colorful outdoor decor. They may share a wide swath on the sidewalk, but they specialize in two very different things. Craft is best known as a quality coffee bar and breakfast spot; in fact, they serve breakfasts until 4 pm, but they also serve burgers for lunch and have a great bar with specialty cocktails and craft beers. Lola is all about Mexican fare and margaritas at lunch, but it turns into a full-on fiesta place late night. It's a strange fusion of offerings but it works, and both spots are typically hopping, so make reservations, especially for dinner at Lola. ⊠ *J. E. Irausquin Blvd. 348-A, Palm Beach* ☎ *297/586–6999* ⊕ *www.craftaruba.com.*

★ Gusto

DANCE CLUBS | Definitely Aruba's most cosmopolitan high-octane dance club, Gusto is where master bartenders show off excellent flair skills while serving up fabulous cocktails to pretty people who want to party late into the night. The island's hottest DJs and a dazzling light show keep the dancing going nonstop. Late-night happy hour is from 9 to 11 pm. All kinds of special events and theme nights add to Gusto's allure, as does VIP bottle service. ⊠ *J. E. Irausquin Blvd. 348-A, Palm Beach* ☎ *297/592–8772* ⊕ *www.gustoaruba.com* ☾ *Closed Mon.*

The Lobby Bar

GATHERING PLACES | Easy-listening local bands get the party started at the lobby bar in the Aruba Marriott. It's a classy venue and an ideal spot for before or after-dinner drinks with superb signature cocktails like the Aruba Aloe Cocktail. ⊠ *Aruba Marriott Resort & Stellaris Casino, L. G. Smith Blvd. 101, Palm Beach* ☎ *297/586– 9000* ⊕ *www.marriott.com.*

★ Lobby Bar and Restaurant

COCKTAIL LOUNGES | Catering to an older, cosmopolitan crowd, this spot has more of a chic supper club lounge vibe than a dining room, and later in the evening, it morphs into an upscale nightclub. There's an excellent wine list and a choice of indoor or outdoor seating. Live music or a DJ set the scene depending on the night and the hour. ⊠ *J. E. Irausquin Blvd. 348, Palm Beach* ☎ *297/280–5330* ⊕ *www.lobbyaruba.com.*

Local Store

BARS | Contrary to its name, it's not a store but a bar, and a very local one at that. Live local bands, lots of resident partiers, and a laid-back, down-to-earth atmosphere make this the place to kick back and have fun, especially on weekends. Good prices on drinks, huge selection of craft beers, and local Aruban snacks like funchi fries (made from seasoned cornmeal or polenta with a crispy outside and a creamy inside), and over a dozen kinds of artisanal chicken wings attract the tourists, too. And they are also open for breakfast and lunch. ⊠ *Palm Beach 13A, Noord* ☎ *297/586–1414* ⊕ *www.facebook.com/LocalStoreAruba.*

★ MooMba Beach Bar

GATHERING PLACES | As the central party spot on the busiest part of Palm Beach, this open-air bar is famous for its Sunday-night blowouts with big crowds of locals gathering to dance in the sand to live bands or DJs. The barkeeps are mixology masters, and happy hours are very popular. There are early and late drink specials every night except Sunday. The attached restaurant is also a wonderful surf-side spot for breakfast, lunch, and dinner, and there are tables in the sand for romantic dinners before partying. Free Wi-Fi and public outdoor bucket showers are a bonus. ⊠ *J. E. Irausquin Blvd. 230,* ⌖ *Between Holiday Inn and Marriott Surf Club* ☎ *297/586–5365* ⊕ *www.moombabeach.com.*

★ purebeach

BARS | South Beach–style cocktails and tapas and full meals are served in this bar and restaurant in the Divi Phoenix Aruba Resort. It's got a cool, hip vibe by day with a swim-up bar where folks gather at happy hour and it's romantically lit by tiki-torches at night, and there's often live music that draws people onto the large dance floor. Special food nights and weekly specials abound like Taco Tuesdays, Wing Wednesdays, and Slider Thursdays. ⊠ *Divi Phoenix Aruba Resort, J. E. Irausquin Blvd. 75, Palm Beach* ☎ *297/586–6606* ⊕ *www.purebeacharuba.com.*

★ Sopranos Piano Bar

PIANO BARS | With a theme loosely based on the famous HBO TV series, Sopranos has a fun atmosphere with live piano music nightly that encourages the crowd to join in a sing-along. Top-notch barkeeps shake up a big list of creative cocktails, and the top-shelf spirit list is impressive. It's loud and rowdy most nights, but nostalgic and low-key when there are no crowds. A DJ sometimes spins late into the night on weekends. ⊠ *Arawak Garden Mall, L. G. Smith Blvd. 177, Palm Beach* ☎ *297/586–8622* ⊕ *www. sopranospianobararuba.com.*

South Beach
DANCE CLUBS | It might not be located on a beach, but you can expect a South Beach Miami vibe with electronic music, flashy lights, and a big outdoor dance floor with DJs. The party starts late and gets crazier as it gets later, attracting a young hip crowd with bottle service and different special events every night of the week. ⊠ *55D Palm Beach, Noord* ✛ *Just off the strip across from the Hilton (follow your ears)* ☎ *297/737–0001* ⊕ *www.facebook. com/southbeacharuba.*

Shopping

CIGARS
★ Aruhiba Cigars
TOBACCO | Look for the big red windmill just off Palm Beach to find this little factory kiosk outlet where the owner hand-rolls quality cigars from tobacco grown on Aruba. Aruhibas have become as popular as Cubans with the island's locals, and some might say, on par with those from Havana. They are also a legal option for visitors seeking cigars to bring back to the United States. ⊠ *Historic Red Windmill, J. E. Irausquin Blvd. 330* ☎ *297/593-6177* ⊕ *www. facebook.com/aruhibacigars* ⊙ *Closed Sat. and Sun.*

Captian Jack Liquor & Cigars
OTHER SPECIALTY STORE | Right on the Palm Beach strip, this store specializes in a wide selection of quality liquors and cigars. ⊠ *La Hacienda Mall, J. E. Irausquin Blvd. 382, Palm Beach* ☎ *297/280– 1142* ⊕ *captian-jack-aruba-liquor-cigar-wine.business.site.*

GIFTS AND SOUVENIRS
★ The Juggling Fish
JEWELRY & WATCHES | This whimsical shop just off the sand is really two separate entities. One side is Juggling Fish Swimwear, a comprehensive selection of quality bathing suits and beach accessories for the entire family, and the other side is dedicated to a selection of creative and unique gifts and souvenirs including avant-garde jewelry and handcrafted items. The staff is warm and friendly, and a portion of all proceeds goes to community programs and charities. ⊠ *Playa Linda Beach Resort, Palm Beach* ☎ *297/592–7802* ⊕ *www.thejugglingfish.com.*

★ T. H. Palm & Company
ANTIQUES & COLLECTIBLES | With an eclectic collection of upscale and exclusive items curated from all over the world by the owner, this unique boutique offers everything from top-line fashions for men and women, including footwear, handcrafted jewelry, and

accessories, to art deco items for the home and novelty gifts for pets. It's a very popular spot for locals to buy gifts as well as for visitors to buy one-of-a-kind souvenirs. A portion of all proceeds goes to the community through a special give-back program. ⊠ *J. E. Irausquin Blvd. 87, Palm Beach* ☎ *297/592–7804* ⊕ *www. thpalmandcompany.com.*

JEWELRY

★ Shiva's Gold and Gems

JEWELRY & WATCHES | A reputable family-run business with shops throughout the Caribbean, this Palm Beach Plaza location saves shoppers from heading to Oranjestad for the type of top-quality diamonds and jewelry downtown is famous for (though there is a location downtown as well). Luxury watches, precious gems, gold, silver, and more are first-rate here, and this is the only store on Aruba that belongs to the Leading Jewelers of the World, which has fewer than 100 retail members. ⊠ *Palm Beach Plaza, L. G. Smith 95, Palm Beach* ☎ *297/583-4011* ⊕ *www.shivasjewelers. com.*

MALLS AND MARKETPLACES

The Cove Mall

MALL | Lively, trendy, fun, fusion, and metamorphosis seem to be the theme of the island's newest cosmopolitan corner of dining and nightlife. It's an entire block of cool new spots that allows you to take your tastebuds on an international tour. You can choose from Asian, Mexican, French, Italian, Greek, and there's even a French bakery that turns into a hot stone steak grill and raw bar at night and a pancake factory that morphs into a clubby dining spot and terrace bar. And looking for craft beer and authentic Aruban comfort food? It's there, too! Nightclubs and VIP rooms are also in the same one block, two-story complex. They also have the island's only rooftop bar/dining spot with private cabanas The Vue on top. It's become the Palm Beach strip's anchor of action, and an excellent spot to start off an electric night on foot. ⊠ *J. E. Irausquin Blvd. 384 A, Unit 5, Palm Beach* ✛ *Across the street from Holiday Inn* ☎ *297/744–9194* ⊕ *www.facebook.com/ thecovearuba.*

Palm Beach Plaza

MALL | **FAMILY** | This modern multistory air-conditioned mall offers fashion, tech, electronics, jewelry, souvenirs, and more. Entertainment includes glow-in-the-dark bowling and local festivals and events like fashion shows. Dining includes a food court and stand-alone restaurants like the new Iguana Joe's. Free Wi-Fi

and parking are a bonus, too. ⊠ *L. G. Smith Blvd. 95, Palm Beach* ☎ *297/586–0045* ⊕ *www.facebook.com/PalmBeachPlazaMall.*

★ Paseo Herencia

MALL | FAMILY | A gorgeous, old-fashioned colonial-style courtyard and clock tower encase souvenir and specialty shops, cinemas, dining spots, cafés, and bars. Just off Palm Beach, this low-rise alfresco mall is famous for its nightly "liquid fireworks" shows—neon-lit water fountains waltz to music in a choreographed dance. Visitors can enjoy it for free from an outdoor amphitheater where many cultural events take place, and there's an Aruban walk of fame here. There's also a fancy carousel for children. New dining outlets line the outside street entrances now, too, like Sibarita Cafe-Bar, *a new picnic terrace, and some cool new food truck–style kiosks offering authentic Aruban snacks.* ⊠ *J. E. Irausquin Blvd. 382, Palm Beach* ☎ *297/586–6533* ⊕ *www.paseoherencia. com.*

PERFUMES AND COSMETICS

★ Maggy's Perfumery and Salon

PERFUME | A true local success story, this is one of the four locations in a local chain that began as a small salon in San Nicolas and evolved into a major perfumery with salons and stores. Though the original Maggy has since passed, the business she began in 1969 is still going strong with her daughter at the helm and many family members still running the business. Quality perfumes and beauty products, as well as health and beauty care services are to be found at all outlets. She also has an online shop now, too. ⊠ *Paseo Herencia, L. G. Smith Blvd. 382, Palm Beach* ☎ *297/529–2118* ⊕ *www.maggysaruba.com.*

SPAS

Eforea Spa

SPAS | Hilton's answer to Zen incarnate, the soothing white seafront building beckons you to enter a world of relaxing signature "journeys" in a Japanese-inspired enclave. Treatments include both the typical and avant-garde, and there are options for both women and men, as well as special seaside massages for couples. There's also a stellar water circuit and full-service beauty salon on-site. Their signature massage includes Aruban aloe, local rum and hot black beach stones, and they also offer an interesting massage that includes vibrational sound therapy. ⊠ *Hilton Aruba Resort, J. E. Irausquin Blvd. 81, Palm Beach* ☎ *297/526–6052* ⊕ *www3.hilton.com.*

Mandara Spa

SPAS | Aruba Marriott's Mandara Spa was created along a Balinese theme and offers specialty Indonesian-style treatments that incorporate the *boreh* (a traditional warm healing pack of special spices) followed by an Aruba-inspired wrap using local aloe and cucumber. The menu also lists a wide variety of skin and body treatments for both women and men, and there's a full-service hair and nail salon, ideal for a wedding party. Honeymooners and couples will appreciate special packages that include private couple's treatment rooms, extra-large whirlpool baths, and Vichy showers. ⊠ *Aruba Marriott Resort & Stellaris Casino, L. G. Smith Blvd. 101, Palm Beach* ☎ *297/520–6750* ⊕ *www.mandaraspa.com.*

★ Pure Indulgence Spa

SPAS | Divi Aruba Phoenix's gorgeous glassed-in multilevel spa has the island's only sea view mani-pedi treatment room (the loft) and has been recently renovated to include an inviting outdoor terrace lounge as a spot to sip your welcome mimosas upon arrival. The Pure Couple's Escape signature treatment includes massage and time spent in a private Lover's Suite replete with whirlpool baths, a steam room, and premium Hansgrohe rain showers. They also offer hot stone and prenatal treatments and a wide range of facials and body renewal packages. ⊠ *Divi Phoenix Aruba Beach Resort, J. E. Irausquin Blvd. 75, Palm Beach* ☎ *297/586–6606* ⊕ *www.purespaaruba.com.*

★ The Ritz-Carlton Spa

SPAS | Upscale pampering and top-notch service is the hallmark of this massive seafront emporium with 13 treatment rooms, a full-service salon, a soothing indoor water therapy pool and an adjoining fitness center with daily classes, including yoga and personal trainers. Signature treatments feature local island ingredients like aloe, divi-divi tree oil, and local coffee (for scrubs), and there's a good selection of treatments for men. On arrival to the island the Jet Lag massage is highly recommended and their "Divi Divi" massage is not to be missed—it was specially developed by their own local therapists incorporating a variety of soothing techniques and oil derived from the local watapana tree. ⊠ *Ritz-Carlton Aruba, L. G. Smith Blvd. 107, Palm Beach* ☎ *297/527–2525* ⊕ *www.ritzcarlton.com* ⊙ *Closed Mon. and Tues.*

ZoiA Spa

SPAS | This luxurious full-service oasis named after the Papiamento word for balance offers treatments indoor and out, and focuses on using Aruba's natural resources for rejuvenation as much as

Many Aruba resorts have thier own spas providing body treatments and massages.

possible—ingredients like red mud, seaweed, and aloe. Their latest unique signature treatments take place right in the water in their new adults-only Trankilo pool facing the sea. "Massage den Awa" is the solo treatment, or you can do it in tandem with your partner with their "Trankilo Couples Devotion" for pure floating bliss. Their express mani-pedis are also very popular, and they offer a full range of hair care in their salon, too. ⊠ *Hyatt Regency Aruba Beach Resort & Casino, J. E. Irausquin Blvd. 85, Palm Beach* ☎ *297/586–1234* ⊕ *www.hyatt.com* ☾ *Closed Sun.*

🎟 Performing Arts

FILM
Caribbean Cinemas VIP
FILM | FAMILY | Ideal for the rare rainy day, or just for something different than the beach, catch a first-run flick in air-conditioned comfort at this ultramodern venue with six stadium seating auditoriums. The fully reclinable leather seats with lots of space between the rows make it even more inviting for a family outing. *It opens at 5 pm weekdays, and 2 pm on weekends.* ⊠ *Paseo Herencia, J.E. Irausquin Blvd. 382A, Palm Beach* ☎ *297/582–3693* ⊕ *www.facebook.com/caribbeancinemasaruba.*

Western Tip (California Dunes)

No trip to Aruba is complete without a visit to the California Lighthouse, and it's also worth exploring the rugged area of the island's western tip. This is the transition point between Aruba's calmer and rougher coasts. Malmok Beach and Arashi Beach are popular with locals and excellent spots for grabbing dramatic sunset photos.

Sights

★ Alto Vista Chapel
NOTABLE BUILDING | Meaning "high view," Alto Vista was built in 1750 as the island's first Roman Catholic Church. The simple yellow-and-orange structure stands out in bright contrast to its stark desertlike surroundings, and its elevated location affords a wonderful panoramic view of the northwest coast. Restored in 1953, it still holds regular services today and also serves as the culmination point of the annual walk of the cross at Easter. You will see small signposts guiding the faithful to the Stations of the Cross all along the winding road to its entrance. This landmark is a typical stop on most island tours. ■ **TIP→ Make sure to buy coconut water from the famous coconut man out front.** ⊠ *Alto Vista Rd., Noord* ✛ *Follow the rough, winding dirt road that loops around the island's northern tip, or from the hotel strip, take Palm Beach Rd. through three intersections and watch for the asphalt road to the left.*

★ California Lighthouse
LIGHTHOUSE | **FAMILY** | Built in 1910, the landmark lighthouse on the island's eastern tip is open to the public, and visitors can climb the spiral stairs to discover a fabulous panoramic view. Declared a national monument in 2015, the lighthouse was named after the merchant ship *California,* which sunk nearby, the tragedy that inspired its construction. ⊠ *2 Hudishibana, Westpunt* ☎ *297/699–0995* ➲ *$5.*

Beaches

★ Arashi Beach
BEACH | This is the local favorite, a half-mile stretch of gleaming white sand with rolling surf and great snorkeling. It can get busy on weekends—especially on Sunday—with local families bringing their own picnics, and visitors have discovered a cool little beach bar called Arashi Beach Shack there with great food, drinks, and

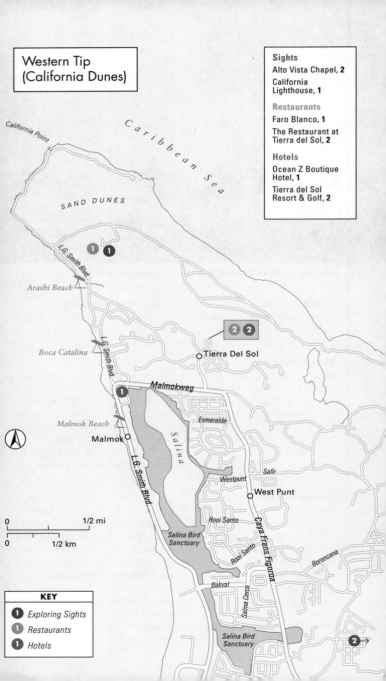

Western Tip
(California Dunes)

Sights
Alto Vista Chapel, **2**
California Lighthouse, **1**

Restaurants
Faro Blanco, **1**
The Restaurant at Tierra del Sol, **2**

Hotels
Ocean Z Boutique Hotel, **1**
Tierra del Sol Resort & Golf, **2**

California Point

C a r i b b e a n   S e a

SAND DUNES

L.G. Smith Blvd.

Arashi Beach

Boca Catalina

L.G. Smith Blvd.

2 **2**

Tierra Del Sol

Malmokweg

1

Malmok Beach

Esmeralda

Salina

Malmok

L.G. Smith Blvd.

Westpunt

Safir

West Punt

Rooi Santo

0   1/2 mi

0   1/2 km

Salina Bird Sanctuary

Rooi Santo

Caya Frans Figaroa

Boroncana

Bakval

Salina Cerca

Salina Bird Sanctuary

2

KEY

1 *Exploring Sights*

1 *Restaurants*

1 *Hotels*

Alto Vista Chapel, on the windy northwest coast of Aruba, was built in 1750.

lounge and beach umbrella rentals. **Amenities:** food and drink; toilets; parking (free). **Best for:** swimming; snorkeling; walking. ⊠ *Malmokweg* ✛ *West of Malmok Beach, on the west end* ⊕ *www.facebook.com/ArashiBeachShack.*

Boca Catalina
BEACH | A fairly isolated strip off a residential area, this tiny white-sand cove attracts snorkelers with its shallow water filled with fish and cool little caves. Swimmers will also appreciate the calm conditions. There aren't any facilities nearby, just a few public shade palapas but no chairs, so pack provisions and your own snorkel gear. It's popular with locals on weekends. **Amenities:** none. **Best for:** snorkeling; swimming. ⊠ *Malmokweg* ✛ *Between Arashi Beach and Malmok Beach, north of intersection of Rtes. 1B and 2B* ⊕ *www.aruba.com/us/explore/boca-catalina.*

Malmok Beach (*Boca Catalina*)
BEACH | On the northwestern shore, this small, nondescript beach borders shallow waters that stretch 300 yards from shore. There are no snack or refreshment stands, but that might change soon with the addition of a new boardwalk leading from Fisherman's Huts beach (part of the Linear Park project) that is now attracting cyclists, strollers, and runners. Most of the main snorkel boat tours stop here for a dip as well as for its incredible sunsets. There is no easy access into the water from the shore; it's very rocky with sharp cliffs and steep descents. Snorkeling is best done from a boat. **Amenities:** none. **Best for:** solitude; snorkeling; sunsets. ⊠ *J. E. Irausquin Blvd., Malmokweg.*

🍴 Restaurants

Faro Blanco

$$$$ | **ITALIAN** | Next to the iconic California lighthouse in the former lighthouse-keeper's home, this restaurant is best known for its upscale Italian fare and grand open-air terrace overlooking the rugged west coast seascape. The restaurant is open all day, but it's renowned for sunset views, when reservations are a must. **Known for:** filetto alla trattoria steak topped with red wine, brown sugar, spices, oranges, and strawberries; stunning sunset views; classics like osso buco and calamari. ⑤ *Average main: $40* ✉ *California Lighthouse* ☎ *297/586–0786* ⊕ *www.faroblancores-taurant.com.*

The Restaurant at Tierra del Sol

$$$$ | **INTERNATIONAL** | The main restaurant at Tierra del Sol sits next to the cliff-top pool and golf course and offers great views of the northwest coast and the California lighthouse. The atmosphere is very country club, but they have a new great new BBQ Saturday and Sunday brunch/lunch featuring ribs and chicken and comfort food sides. **Known for:** prix-fixe "all u can taste" menu with apps, tapas, and add-ons; great views and romantic candlelight alfresco dining; popular à la carte Sunday brunch. ⑤ *Average main: $65* ✉ *Tierra del Sol Resort* ☎ *297/586–7800* ⊕ *www.tierradelsol.com* ☾ *No dinner Sun. and Mon.*

🛏 Hotels

Ocean Z Boutique Hotel

$$$$ | **HOTEL** | A unique luxury boutique resort far from the touristy fray is across the road from the wild and scenic Malmok Cliffs, offering rooms surrounding a solarium pool as well as a few oceanfront suites. **Pros:** intimate and personal first-rate service; chic solitary escape away from the crowds; gorgeous scenic setting with sea views. **Cons:** not on a beach; not within walking distance to any other dining or shopping; no entertainment. ⑤ *Rooms from: $588* ✉ *L. G. Smith Blvd. 526, Malmokweg* ☎ *297/586–9500* ⊕ *www.oceanzaruba.com* 🛏 *13 rooms* ⏹ *Free Breakfast.*

Tierra del Sol Resort & Golf

$$$ | **RESORT** | More of a sprawling gated community than a resort, these upscale properties range in size from two-bedroom condos and duplex villas to sprawling home-style abodes with pools and manicured lawns, making it the choice of many a visiting celebrity. **Pros:** exclusive private-club vibe; complimentary transportation to

Arashi Beach close by; high level of personalized services availa-ble. **Cons:** not directly on a beach; limited choice of dining; far from shopping and nightlife. ⑤ *Rooms from: $385* ⊠ *Tierra Del Sol, Caya di Solo 10, Noord* ☎ *297/439–8578* ⊕ *www.tierradelsol.com* ⇔ *20 units* �� *No Meals.*

Shopping

There is little shopping on this far end of the island beyond small boutiques in the hotels and local convenience stores.

SPAS
The Spa at Tierra del Sol

SPAS | Expect high-end massages, wraps, scrubs, and skin treat-ments, and a full hair- and nail-care salon (perfect for weddings) at Tierra del Sol's luxury spa. Highlights include the sea-sand detox skin treatment or the private whirlpool where couples can relax with champagne. Non-resort spa guests are welcome to use the fitness center and the resort's cliff-side pool looking out at the California Lighthouse as well. ⊠ *Tierra del Sol, Caya di Solo 10, Noord* ☎ *297/586–7800* ⊕ *www.tierradelsol.com* ☉ *Closed Mon.*

SAN NICOLAS AND SAVANETA

Updated by
Susan Campbell

⊙ Sights   🍴 Restaurants   🛏 Hotels   🛍 Shopping   🍸 Nightlife

★★★★☆   ★★★★★   ★★★★★   ★★★★★   ★★★★★

NEIGHBORHOOD SNAPSHOT

TOP EXPERIENCES

- **Mural Walk:** Take a self-guided (or guided) tour of San Nicolas to view the incredible outdoor art and murals that have rejuvenated the town.
- **Try a Boozer Colada:** Stop by legendary Charlie's Bar to try this potent, signature cocktail and check out the cool collection of items left behind by customers over the past 70 years.
- **Seafood Straight from the Boat:** At Zeerovers in Savaneta, watch fishermen bring in their catch and then pick exactly what you want for lunch.
- **Relax at Baby Beach:** Go snorkeling to really experience all this beach's wonders.
- **Shop Local:** Visit Cosecha Creative Centre for locally made arts and crafts; they even host workshops.
- **Mangel Halto's mangrove canals:** Kayak or paddleboard through the canals' calm waters; don't miss the secluded beach.

GETTING HERE AND AROUND

There is a public bus from downtown Oranjestad to Savaneta and San Nicolas, but it takes a long time. Taxis are pricey, but worth it if you're going for dinner and don't want to drink and drive. Or hire a driver for the day to explore the area.

From downtown Oranjestad, it should take about 15 minutes to drive to Savaneta and about 20–25 minutes to get to San Nicolas.

PLANNING YOUR TIME

Sunday's the most popular beach day for locals, and many shops are closed. The best time to visit San Nicolas and Savaneta is during the day, but Savaneta has great dinner options.

VIEWFINDER

- The giant red anchor outside of Seroe Colorado honoring the seafarers is a popular photo pit stop, and the rugged coastline there offers gorgeous natural vistas; you can also capture stunning shots from Rum Reef's infinity pool overlooking breathtaking Baby Beach. But you need not venture any further than San Nicolas proper for a gazillion exceptional Insta-worthy muses as the entire downtown grid is bedecked with outstanding outdoor murals and art. Explore it on your own or take a guided tour with Aruba Art Fair (⊕ aruba-muraltours.com), the organization that spearheaded the mural movement.

Savaneta, the island's original capital, is historically referred to as Commander's Bay since this is where the first Dutch Commanders resided. Farther south, the little ex-refinery town of San Nicolas is known locally as Sunrise City due to its brilliant sunrises. Today both towns are receiving renewed interest as tourist destinations as they begin to focus more on preserving and promoting the island's history, culture, and art.

Planning

Festivals and Street Parties

Aruba Art Fair

Organized by ArtisA, this annual three-day event takes place each fall when artists from around the world are invited to collaborate on outdoor installations, sculptures, murals, and more throughout San Nicolas. There are workshops with the artists, as well as a Youth Art Fair that showcases the island's young aspiring artists. The event also includes an ArtFashion show that features the most creative works of local designers, and there are special events like pop-up restaurants, culinary art competitions, and lots of music and dancing in the streets. The work left behind from past years has turned the downtown core into a magical maze of outdoor art and will continue to do so for years to come. ⊠ *San Nicolas Promenade* ☎ *297/593–4475* ⊕ *arubaartfair.com.*

Carnival

Most of the main events during the annual Carnival take place in Oranjestad, but San Nicolas is considered to be the birthplace of the island's carnival traditions. Celebrations include a lighting parade, music competitions, and a mini-grande parade the day before the big one in Oranjestad. And this is the only location for Jouvert Morning, the annual sunrise road march that starts at 4 am—another reason the town was dubbed "Sunrise City." The

new Carnival Village in the heart of town now hosts many more events year-round and weekend nights you'll often have small bands outside the colorful little food truck–style kiosks for local's night out. You can also grab some great local food and cold beer there during the day after 11am; there's always at least one of them open. ⊠ *Lagoweg Oranjestad, Aruba, Savaneta*.

San Nicolas

During the oil refinery heyday, Aruba's oldest village was a bus-tling port and the island's economic hub. As demand for oil dwin-dled and tourism rose, attention shifted to Oranjestad and the island's best beaches. The past few years have seen a renaissance in San Nicolas largely due to the improvement of its infrastructure and the beautification of its main streets, which have become an exciting outdoor art district. There are new museums and a cinema, a new carnival village with food kiosks and live music on weekends, and many multiethnic food choices in the downtown and surrounding regions. Rotating street festivals and farmers' markets continue to introduce visitors to the unique charms of Sunrise City, and the legendary Charlie's Bar & Restaurant, a fam-ily-run business that's been around since 1941, continues to draw patrons from around the world. The San Nicolas Cosecha Creative Centre is also a draw for high-end, locally made art and crafts and offers many different art workshops and events that visitors can attend.

The seafront area around Seroe Colorado is earmarked for devel-opment in the very near future, and the Baby Beach area is also being expanded to accommodate more tourism.

👁 Sights

★ ArtisA

ARTS CENTER | Part art gallery, part administrative foundation, ArtisA (Art is Aruba) is responsible for the art and culture revolution in San Nicolas. The foundation displays local art for sale, hosts monthly exhibits for local artists, and is the spot to purchase tickets for the guided Aruba Mural Tours (also available online). They are now hosting art-meets-cuisine special events with local chefs' table din-ners highlighting a showcase inspired by local artists within their space. ⊠ *Bernard van de Veen Zeppenfeldstraat 14, San Nicolas* ✛ *Look for the stunning silver sculpture out front* ☎ *297/593–4475* 🌐 *www.facebook.com/ARTISARUBA* 🕑 *Closed Sun.*

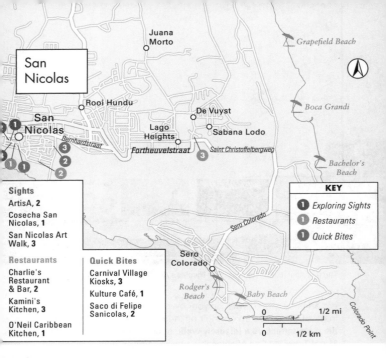

Sights

ArtisA, **2**

Cosecha San Nicolas, **1**

San Nicolas Art Walk, **3**

Restaurants

Charlie's Restaurant & Bar, **2**

Kamini's Kitchen, **3**

O'Neil Caribbean Kitchen, **1**

Quick Bites

Carnival Village Kiosks, **3**

Kulture Café, **1**

Saco di Felipe Sanicolas, **2**

KEY

1 *Exploring Sights*

1 *Restaurants*

1 *Quick Bites*

★ Cosecha San Nicolas

ARTS CENTER | Sister outfit of the downtown location, this arty emporium is a wonderful place to view and purchase high quality made-in-Aruba art, crafts, jewelry, and more. Workshops for all ages are available on a regular basis so you can learn to work with different mediums and create your own unique Aruban souvenirs, too. Special exhibitions and events with local artists occur on a rotating basis as well. ⊠ *Bernard van de Veen Zeppenfeldstraat 20, San Nicolas* ✛ *Look for the giant pink flamingo head on the building* ☎ *297/587–8709* ⊕ *www.arubacosecha.com/cosechacreativecenter* ☉ *Sun. to Wed.* ☞ *Open Thurs.–Sat. 1:30 pm–6:30 pm.*

San Nicolas Art Walk

PUBLIC ART | In the past few years, San Nicolas has seen an extraordinary revitalization and beautification thanks to new art initiatives organized by the local artist's foundation, ArtisA (Art is Aruba). What began as a simple mural project in 2015 has since blossomed into the establishment of an annual Aruba Art Fair whose aim is to create more public art projects. The incredible murals can cover entire buildings, and every year the collection grows. You'll find giant iguanas made from recycled materials, glowing lionfish, 3D installations, interactive art, and many murals.

The beautiful murals found on San Nicolas's Art Walk began in 2015.

It's an easy grid to walk on your own, or you can see where each installation is located on their online map. ■ TIP→ **You can see the installations on a leisurely walk, or on a guided walk with Aruba Mural Tours.** ⊠ *San Nicolas* ⊕ *arubamuraltours.com.*

🔱 Beaches

The beaches surrounding San Nicolas range from pristine soft sand edged by aqua waters to wild and windswept kitesurfing hot spots and romantic yet unswimmable picturesque escapes.

★ **Baby Beach**

BEACH | FAMILY | On the island's eastern tip (near the refinery), this semicircular beach borders a placid bay of turquoise water that's just about as shallow as a wading pool—perfect for families with little ones. A small coral reef basin at the sea's edge offers superb snorkeling, but do not pass the barrier as the current is extremely strong outside the rocks. The JADS dive shop offers snorkel equipment rentals, and this is a popular place to see and swim with sea turtles, too. Rum Reef on one end is a unique adults-only bar and infinity pool overlooking the beach, and on the other end you can rent clamshell shade tents and lounges on the beach from Big Mamma Grill, a family-friendly gathering spot. **Amenities:** food and drink; showers; toilets; parking (free); **Best for:** snorkeling; swimming. ⊠ *Seroe Colorado.*

Bachelor's Beach

BEACH | This eastside beach is known for its white-powder sand. Snorkeling can be good, but bring a guide, and the conditions aren't the best for swimming as the currents can be strong. **Amenities:** none. **Best for:** snorkeling; windsurfing. ⊠ *East end, south of Boca Grandi.*

Boca Grandi

BEACH | This is *the* choice for the island's best kiteboarders and expert windsurfers, even more so than Fisherman's Huts. But the currents are seriously strong, so it's not safe for casual swimming. It's very picturesque, though, and a perfect spot for a picnic. It's a few minutes from San Nicolas proper; look for the big red anchor or the kites in the air. But be forewarned: the conditions are not for amateurs, and there are no lifeguards or facilities nearby should you get into trouble. **Amenities:** parking (free). **Best for:** solitude; walking; windsurfing. ⊠ *San Nicolas ✣ Near Seagrape Grove, on the east end.*

Grapefield Beach

BEACH | Just North of Boca Grandi on the eastern coast, a sweep of blinding-white sand in the shadow of cliffs and boulders is marked by an anchor-shape memorial dedicated to seamen. Pick sea grapes from January to June. Swimming is not recommended as the waves here can be rough. This is not a popular tourist beach, so finding a quiet spot is almost guaranteed, but the downside of this is a complete lack of facilities or nearby refreshments. **Amenities:** none. **Best for:** solitude, picnics. ⊠ *Southwest of San Nicolas, on east end.*

Rodger's Beach

BEACH | **FAMILY** | Near Baby Beach on the island's eastern tip, this beautiful curving stretch of sand is only slightly marred by its proximity to the tanks and towers of the oil refinery at the bay's far side. Look for the stone stairs descending to the sand; the swimming conditions are excellent here. It's usually very quiet during the week, so you might have the beach all to yourself, but it's a local favorite on weekends. Full facilities can be found next door at JADS dive center strip on Baby Beach. **Amenities:** food and drink; toilets; parking (free). **Best for:** swimming; solitude. ⊠ *Seroe Colorado ✣ Next to Baby Beach.*

🍴 Restaurants

During Aruba's oil boom, San Nicolas became a cultural melting pot as many workers brought their own flavors of food to the island. Today, you'll find everything from Jamaican and Trinidadian cuisines to South American and Asian, usually all with an Aruban twist. There is modern urban fare too like barista-style coffees, wraps, and great breakfasts at the new Kulture Cafe at the historic Nicolaas Store. And, for really local fare be sure to seek out the "sacos," a San Nicolas specialty that consists of a brown paper bag filled with finger-licking-good items like ribs, chicken, pork chops, johnnycakes, fried potatoes, corn on the cob, or plantains. Sacos are so well-known that locals and repeat visitors in-the-know often make a special trip from the other end of the island for them, usually with a stop at Saco di Felipe, a hole-in-the-wall spot that's been in business for six decades. Yes, its greasy, but that's the point, and it's addictive. Just don't ask for cutlery, as you're supposed to eat it all with your hands.

★ Charlie's Restaurant & Bar

$$$ | **CARIBBEAN** | Since 1941, Charlie's Bar has been the heart and soul of San Nicolas, famous for its interior decorated with the eclectic bric-a-brac left behind by decades of international visitors. But it also serves surprisingly good food, including superb fresh fish and shrimp, as well as killer steaks. **Known for:** third-generation owner named Charles; a legendary San Nicolas institution; "Boozer Coladas," the signature drink. ⑤ *Average main: $25* ⊠ *Zeppenfeldstraat 56, San Nicolas* ☎ *297/584–5086* ⊕ *www.facebook. com/charliesbararuba* ⊙ *Closed Sun.*

★ Kamini's Kitchen

$$ | **CARIBBEAN** | Housed in a cheery blue and green cottage, this charming spot is run by Kamini Kurvink who combines her Trinidadian heritage with local flavors to create unique Caribbean comfort food. Fish, seafood, and meat dishes are served with a spicy flair due to Kamini's secret signature hot sauces. **Known for:** very warm, welcoming, and friendly staff and owner; hearty portions of homemade Caribbean specialties like goat curry and chicken roti; a great selection of vegetarian options. ⑤ *Average main: $12* ⊠ *De Vuyst 41B, San Nicolas* ☎ *297/587–1398* ⊕ *www.facebook.com/ KaminisKitchen* ⊙ *Closed Tues.*

O'Niel Caribbean Kitchen

$$ | **CARIBBEAN** | **FAMILY** | Right smack in the middle of the exciting San Nicolas art walk, O'Niel's is a warm and welcoming eatery that's an ideal spot to get your Jamaican jerk on. Real deal

Baby Beach is a great spot for families.

Jamaican dishes like ackee with salt fish and oxtail with beans are menu favorites, but there are also many local Aruban specialties like goat stew and fresh local fish and seafood. **Known for:** local favorite; coconut-infused dishes like shrimp or chicken with rum and sweet chili sauce; real-deal Jamaican specialties like ackee with salt fish. ⑤ *Average main: $15* ✉ *Bernard van de Veen Zeppenfeldstraat 15, San Nicolas* ☎ *297/584–8700* ⊕ *www.facebook.com/OnielCaribbeanKitchen297* ⊗ *Closed Mon.*

☕ Coffee and Quick Bites

Carnival Village Kiosks
$ | CARIBBEAN | Colorful wooden kiosks fill the area around the outside of the fenced-in square with folks offering food truck–style fare and cold drinks. They are not all open every day, but there is usually one open at any given time, and only after 11 am. **Known for:** most are licensed to serve beer as well; authentic local fare like johnnycakes and salt fish; great prices for big portions. ⑤ *Average main: $8* ✉ *Lagoweg, San Nicolaas* ▭ *No credit cards.*

★ Kulture Café
$ | CAFÉ | The new café in the beautifully restored historic Nicolaas Store in the heart of downtown San Nicolas serves up great barista-style hot and iced coffees and snacks. With seating indoors or out, this is an ideal pit stop before or after exploring the outdoor art. **Known for:** ice cream and decadent desserts like caramel sea

Seroe Colorado: A Ghost Town

This surreal ghost town was originally built as a community for American oil workers who came to run the Lago Refinery in the 1950s. There were 700 residents, an English-language school, a social club, a beach club, a hospital, a local newspaper, and a bowling alley.

Today, organ-pipe cacti form the backdrop for the sedate whitewashed cottages. And ground has been broken for a new adults-only inclusive hotel by AMResorts slated to open in 2022.

salt cheesecake; excellent wraps and paninis; great local and American-style breakfasts. $ *Average main: $7* ⊠ *V/D Veen Zeppenveldstraat 27, San Nicolaas* ☎ *297/280–5566* ⊕ *www.facebook.com/Kulturecafearuba.*

Saco di Felipe Sanicolas
$ | **CARIBBEAN** | This hole-in-the-wall is *the* place for the best "sacos," paper bags full of fried chicken, ribs, chops, plantains, fries, and johnnycakes. It's the perfect snack before, or after, a night out. **Known for:** all fried fare, greasy but good, an especially hearty snack for after bar hopping; sacos are known as a "heart attack in a bag" but it's so worth it. $ *Average main: $10* ⊠ *St Maarten Straat,* ⊗ *No lunch* ⊟ *No credit cards.*

Hotels

Places to stay are few and far between in San Nicolas proper, but that might change in the next few years as there are big plans for an area that once housed Americans working at the oil refinery in Seroe Colorado in the '40s and '50s. With that said, if you really want to be in the area, you might find an Airbnb close to Baby Beach or Rodgers Beach. The closest boutique hotels are in Savaneta.

Nightlife

Unless there's a street festival going on, San Nicolas's nightlife is confined to a few local spots that occasionally have live music outside like the new Carnival Village, but the town is not really a place for barhopping as most of the little bars double as brothels that are part of the small but legal red-light district. However, when there is a scheduled street festival or annual event like the Aruba

Art Fair, it's very safe for everyone, including families, after dark, and the events are well worth attending. There is also a modern new cinema for first-run movies if you want to escape the heat for awhile after a day touring or time at the beach.

Performing Arts

Principal Cinema

FILM | After nearly three decades, locals are delighted to have a modern cinema in San Nicolas again. The air-conditioned cinema is state-of-the-art with large screens, VIP seats, and a modern concession stand. It's an ideal place to catch a flick before or after Baby Beach. ⊠ *Stuyvesant Straat 20, San Nicolas* ⚓ *In the main promenade downtown* ☎ *297/523–6844* ⊕ *www.themoviesaruba. com/sannicolas.*

Shopping

There are lots of mom-and-pop shops, clothing stores, small department stores, mini-markets and grocery outlets, modern pharmacies, and a few hardware stores scattered about, so you'll have no problem finding anything you forgot to bring out on a day trip. If you're seeking unique souvenirs, then San Nicolas is the place for locally made arts and crafts.

Savaneta

It might be hard to believe that this sleepy little community on the southeastern coast was once Aruba's first capital city, but it was, until 1797. The Dutch commanders made their residences here and this is where the island's first stone house was built as the governor's residence. Today, this popular fishing spot is very much a local neighborhood with a laid-back, easy vibe and some new boho-chic places to stay. Cosmopolitan cafés are sidling up to heritage buildings, and new ecoactivities and arty pastimes are also taking hold. There is talk of a new museum to trace the village's interesting past. Savaneta is also home to the island's only Olympic-size public swimming pool and the spot where they train their Olympic contenders—the island sent swimmers to the summer Olympics in 2016 and 2021. It's also home to the Royal Netherlands Navy, the Netherlands Marine Corps, and the Netherlands Coastguard, so don't be surprised to see their ships gliding by often and close to shore, and don't be shy to wave... they like that.

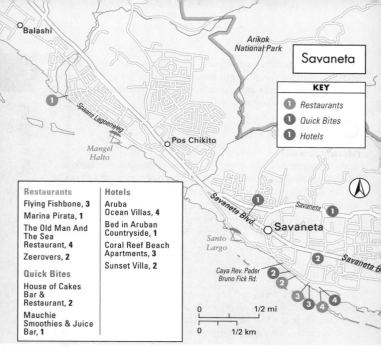

Savaneta

KEY

1 Restaurants
1 Quick Bites
1 Hotels

Restaurants
Flying Fishbone, **3**
Marina Pirata, **1**
The Old Man And The Sea Restaurant, **4**
Zeerovers, **2**

Quick Bites
House of Cakes Bar & Restaurant, **2**
Mauchie Smoothies & Juice Bar, **1**

Hotels
Aruba Ocean Villas, **4**
Bed in Aruban Countryside, **1**
Coral Reef Beach Apartments, **3**
Sunset Villa, **2**

 Beaches

Savaneta is not really a beach community, as most of the swimming is done by jumping off a dock or deck, so don't except to see long strands of soft white sand like other parts of the island. Mangel Halto, and the little stretch at Santo Largo, are the exceptions.

Mangel Halto (*Savaneta Beach*)
BEACH | With a purposely scuttled boat wreck near the coast, and a lot to see outside the bay, this is one of the most popular spots for shore diving, but be aware that currents are strong once you're outside the cove. It's also popular for picnics, and a wooden dock and stairs into the ocean make getting into the water easy. Sea kayak tours depart from here, and some outfits offer power snorkeling and regular snorkeling as well. There are stores within easy walking distance for food and drink. There are very few palapas, but you can take shade under the many trees and mangroves.
Amenities: none. **Best for:** snorkeling; swimming; water sports.
⊠ *Savaneta* ⊕ *Between Savaneta proper and Pos Chiquito.*

Santo Largo
BEACH | A small pristine beach in between Mangel Halto and Gouverner's Bay (just before Flying Fishbone) makes an ideal picnic

spot far away from the crowds. Swimming conditions are good—thanks to shallow water edged by white-powder sand—but there are no facilities and virtually no shade. **Amenities:** none. **Best for:** swimming. ⊠ *San Nicolas.*

 Restaurants

Little cafés, snack bars, and Asian food takeouts can be found around the town, but for the best eats and fine dining head to the few waterfront spots peppered around the coastline.

★ Flying Fishbone

$$$$ | **INTERNATIONAL** | Opened in 1977, this was the first restaurant in Aruba to offer feet-in-the-water dining, and that's why the legendary landmark is so worth the trek out to Savaneta for its insanely romantic seaside setting. An international menu is designed to please all palates, but the real culinary draw is fish straight from the island's most famous local fisherman's pier located a few doors over. **Known for:** tables set right in the ocean; "Savaneta's Seafood History" featuring the very local catch of the day; personal flambéed baked Alaska. ⑤ *Average main: $40* ⊠ *Savaneta 344, Savaneta* ☎ *297/584–2506* ⊕ *www.flyingfishbone.com* ⊙ *No Lunch.*

Marina Pirata

$$$ | **CARIBBEAN** | **FAMILY** | Locals and regular visitors in the know flock to this off-the-radar boathouse-style restaurant for fresh fish and seafood, as well as the melt-in-your-mouth fillet. Spectacular sunset views are a given, and kids love seeing the abundant fish swimming all around the pier and illuminated at night with underwater lights. **Known for:** great place for group celebrations; many squid dishes; fresh local lobster served different ways. ⑤ *Average main: $25* ⊠ *Spanish Waters, Spaans Lagoenweg 4, Savaneta* ☎ *297/585–7150* ⊕ *www.facebook.com/Marinapirataaruba* ⊙ *Closed Tues. No lunch Mon.*

★ The Old Man And The Sea Restaurant

$$$$ | **CARIBBEAN** | The signature restaurant of Aruba Ocean Villas resort is tiny; there are only seven tables plus one incredible overwater palapa for private dining that's especially popular for proposals. The aura is romantic, toes-in-the-sand adults-only dining with soft music and twinkling lights, and though the restaurant and tiki bar are reserved for guests for breakfast and lunch, off-property visitors can reserve dinner here if tables are available. **Known for:** local favorite desserts like quesillo (flan) and cashew nut cake; locally caught and perfectly prepared lobster and surf and turf; excellent cuts of meat like filet mignon with

creative sauces. $ *Average main: $55* ✉ *Savaneta 356A, Savaneta* ☎ *297/584–3434* ⊕ *www.arubaoceanvillas.com/restaurant.*

Zeerovers

$ | **CARIBBEAN** | **FAMILY** | With a name that means "pirates" in Dutch, this small restaurant sits right on the Savaneta pier, where the local fishermen bring in their daily catch. The menu is basic: the day's fish and other seafood fried almost as soon as it's lifted out of the boat, with sides of local staples like plantains that you can chase down with cold local beer. **Known for:** picturesque sea view and sunsets; freshest fish on the island; lively local hangout. $ *Average main: $10* ✉ *Savaneta Pier, Savaneta 270A, Savaneta* ☎ *297/584–8401* ⊕ *www.facebook.com/zeerovers* ⊗ *Closed Mon. and Tues.* ▭ *No credit cards.*

Coffee and Quick Bites

House of Cakes Bar & Restaurant

$ | **INTERNATIONAL** | About 10 minutes past the airport en route to San Nicolas, this cheery little spot serves a lot more than baked goods and authentic Aruban cakes by the slice. They are also popular for their breakfasts, occasional weekend BBQs, and great snack platters to go. **Known for:** local fare lunch specials; all-you-can eat weekend breakfasts; fresh cakes, pastries, and sweets. $ *Average main: $10* ✉ *Rte. 1, Savaneta* ☎ *297/584–2323* ⊕ *houseofcakes.business.site.*

Mauchie Smoothies & Juice Bar

$ | **INTERNATIONAL** | This colorful roadside stand, just before the Savaneta turn, has excellent smoothies and fresh juices, as well as decadent shakes, burgers, and quesadillas. There are great organic herbal remedies made from local produce, too. **Known for:** great smoothies made with local produce; hearty burgers and quesadillas at a good price; healthy organic and locally sourced juices. $ *Average main: $8* ✉ *New Winter Garden, Savaneta 87, Savaneta* ☎ *297/584–7115* ⊕ *www.facebook.com/ mauchismoothies.*

Hotels

Most of the accommodations in the Savaneta area are private home rentals or rooms available via Airbnb, but there are a few notable exceptions.

★ Aruba Ocean Villas

$$$$ | **RESORT** | A secret collection of stunning adults-only luxury villas, some Tahitian overwater palapa bungalows, some on the

Located in Savaneta, Mangel Halto is a popular spot for shore diving and picnics.

beach, some Bali bamboo style, and one two-story treehouse, are all gorgeously hand-decorated by owner artist Osyth Henriquez with treasures curated from her world travels. **Pros:** far from the tourist fray; insanely romantic setting, ideal for honeymoons; luxurious elite vibe yet friendly staff. **Cons:** no pool in common area; a car is needed; little entertainment. $ *Rooms from: $650* ⊠ *Savaneta 356A, Savaneta* ✛ *A few doors down from the Flying Fishbone restaurant* ☎ *297/594–1815, 844/920–1381 in the U.S.* ⊕ *www.arubaoceanvillas.com* 🛌 *8 villas* ⦿ *Free Breakfast.*

Bed in Aruban Countryside
$ | **APARTMENT** | In this charming complex, brightly colored cottage-style studios have their own kitchens, and guests have access to a garden patio and gazebos, a modern barbecue, and a large communal table—plus it's only a five-minute drive to Mangel Halto Beach. **Pros:** budget-friendly, clean, and well kept; a great stay for animal lovers; authentic local experience. **Cons:** you need a car to get around; not on a beach; no dining on-site. $ *Rooms from: $60* ⊠ *Seroe Alejandro 6, Savaneta* ☎ *297/593–2933* 🛌 *4 studio apartments* ⦿ *No Meals.*

Coral Reef Beach Apartments
$ | **HOTEL** | This beachfront complex with apartment-style rooms has a fully stocked communal kitchen for guests to self-cater and a tiny private beach and deck with an abundance of hammocks and picnic tables. **Pros:** maid service and Wi-Fi included; bright, fresh rooms, some with great sea views; two large suites are great for families on a budget. **Cons:** communal kitchen is not

always convenient for everyone; rooms do not have hot water; not all rooms have sea views. $ *Rooms from: $204* ✉ *Savaneta 344A, Savaneta* ☎ *297/584–7764* ⊕ *www.coralreefbeachapartments.com* ⤵ *8 units* ⦿ *No Meals.*

★ Sunset Villa

$$$$ | **HOUSE** | **FAMILY** | Formerly called Casa Alistaire, and once home to the owner of Aruba Ocean Villas, this incredible semi-overwater complex holds all kinds of surprises like a massive crystal chandelier, a grand piano, a huge deck, a restaurant-size fully equipped kitchen, and four bedrooms (sleeps 8 adults), all decked out with their own theme. **Pros:** great swimming and snorkeling right off the deck; spacious retreat full of unique decor and luxury amenities; housekeeping available. **Cons:** far from shopping and nightlife (you need a car); no laundry facilities; families with toddlers should be vigilant on the deck as it has no rails. $ *Rooms from: $1299* ✉ *Savaneta 258B, Savaneta* ☎ *297/584–3434* ⊕ *www.arubaoceanvillas.com/sunset-villa* ⤵ *1 unit* ⦿ *No Meals.*

Shopping

There's not much shopping per se around Savaneta save a handful of mini-markets and general supply stores. Occasional pop-up festivals with local farmers and craftspeople appear, but are not regularly scheduled.

🏃 Activities

SPAS

★ Indira Skin Care

SPAS | An enchanting surprise awaits on the road to San Nicolas just before the Savaneta turnoff in the form of this full-service spa and art gallery owned by the artist Merveline Geerman, who also happens to be a licensed skin-care specialist and masseuse. A full range of treatments are available including makeup and manipedis. ✉ *Savaneta 91, Savaneta* ☎ *297/584–6263* ⊙ *Closed Sun.*

ARIKOK NATIONAL PARK AND ENVIRONS

Updated by
Susan Campbell

👁 Sights 🍴 Restaurants 🛏 Hotels 🛒 Shopping 🍸 Nightlife

★★★★★ ★☆☆☆☆ ☆☆☆☆☆ ☆☆☆☆☆ ☆☆☆☆☆

NEIGHBORHOOD SNAPSHOT

TOP EXPERIENCES

- **Go Wild:** Discover the park's untamed wilderness with a guided tour on foot or by vehicle.
- **Cool off in "Conchi":** Join a jeep safari trek to swim in the surreal natural pool.
- **Hike the Haystack:** Climb Mt. Hooiberg—the island's second-highest peak—for bragging rights and a great view.
- **Climb Casabari:** Discover odd rock formations that look like something out of *The Flintstones*.
- **Meet Cool Critters:** Visit the Donkey Sanctuary and the Ostrich Farm to make new animal friends.

GETTING HERE AND AROUND

A few main highways lead to the national park entrance. Depending on where you are coming from—Palm Beach, Eagle Beach, or Oranjestad—it's best to check a map for the fastest route. It's also best to take a guided tour of the park to get your bearings as it can be an unforgiving outback in many places, and definitely requires a four-wheel-drive vehicle. The Arubiana mapping app (⊕ *www.arubiana.com*) is very helpful and works offline as well.

PLANNING YOUR TIME

The interior region is best explored during daylight hours, as there's little to do and not well-lit at night. The park closes at 4 pm; overnight camping is not allowed. If you plan on hiking in the park, go early because it gets very hot in the afternoon, and there's little shade.

VIEWFINDER

- One of the most popular spots for stunning shots in Arikok National Park has always been the natural pool or *conchi*, but the photo ops at Dos Playa are pretty spectacular, too. Snap a selfie there with the dramatic contours and contrasts of crashing aqua waves, white sand coves, and craggy cliffs as your backdrop. And though the interiors of the caves are also Insta-worthy, no flash photography is permitted. Also note that drone photography isn't permitted within the park so as not to disturb nature.

First-time visitors are often surprised to discover how desertlike the other side of Aruba becomes once away from the landscaped grounds of the resorts with their swaying palms and brightly colored blooms. The island's interior and northeast coast are arid, rocky, and wild. But they have their own unique beauty, and are well worth exploring for surreal scenic vistas, romantic wave-whipped cliffs, and vast expanses of untouched wilderness.

Arikok National Park takes up approximately 20% of the island and is fiercely protected due to its fragile ecosystem; visitors must pay a park fee and abide by park rules in order to enjoy it. And although off-roading is allowed, first-time visitors should take a guided tour and learn the rules of the road, as driving on the dunes and on the beaches is highly discouraged. Within the park there are many surprises beyond cacti forests, dry riverbeds, and twisted divi-divi trees. There are cool caves like Fontein and Guadarikiri, a remote natural pool known as "Conchi," and Mt. Jamanota, the island's highest peak. Meandering goats and donkeys are common, but the park's elusive wildlife *is* easier to discover with the help of a guide. Park rangers offer free tours and man the entrances to the caves to enlighten about their ancient history.

Surrounding the park in the interior are neighborhoods worth exploring if you want to see how the locals live, like in Santa Cruz where you should sleuth out the numerous "snacks"—small food outlets that serve great homemade fare at very low prices.

■ TIP➔ **Make sure you have cash. These spots don't take credit cards.**

There's also Paradera, a small interior neighborhood where you'll find three natural attractions—the Casibari and Ayo rock formations and Mt. Hooiberg ("The Haystack")—all worth a visit on their own.

Arikok National Park

Aruba's national park encompasses 7,907 acres. Guests can explore the island's untamed wilderness by vehicle, horseback, or guided tour with a park ranger. The park's natural wonders include cool caves, a remote natural pool to swim and snorkel in, as well as the island's tallest peak, Mt. Jamanota, which is only recommended for experienced hikers. It also extends now to the Spanish Lagoon region to protect its waterways and mangroves.

Sights

★ Arikok National Park

NATIONAL PARK | Covering almost 20% of the island's landmass, this protected preserve of arid, cacti-studded outback has interesting nature and wildlife if you know where to look. There are close to 30 miles of hiking trails within the park zone including a trek up Mt. Jamanota, the island's highest peak. Hiking maps for all levels of hikers are free at the visitor center, and in-depth maps of the park and its attractions are also available for download online at their website. It's highly recommended to take a guided tour on foot or by vehicle, as the roads can be very rough in some places; there are plenty of excursions by ATV, UTV, Jeep safaris, and more. A guided preview of what you can expect will help you if you want to return in your own rental car as well, but keep in mind that a 4x4 vehicle is a must and all visitors must pay a park entrance fee, which helps fund the park's ecoconservation. Some trails lead to glorious seaside coastal views, but a guided tour will help you understand the significance of the region and help you find attractions like the caves on the northeastern coast. There are no facilities past the visitor center so bring plenty of water and sunscreen and wear good shoes, as the terrain is very rocky. A new region near Spanish Lagoon has also been added recently as part of its protected area due to the importance of its freshwater canals and mangrove forests, but it is closer to Savaneta on the southwest coast, and not within the original park confines. ■TIP→ **You can book free guided hikes with a park ranger by phone or email, but must reserve 48 hours in advance.** ⊠ *San Fuego 70, Arikok National Park* ☎ *297/585–1234* ⊕ *www.arubanationalpark. org* ⊠ *$11* ⊙ *Park closes at 4 pm daily.*

Arikok Visitor Center

VISITOR CENTER | **FAMILY** | At the park's main entrance, Arikok Visitor Center houses offices, restrooms, and food facilities. All visitors must stop here upon entering so that officials can manage the

The Natural Pool, or "conchi", was once a secret spot due to its remote location.

traffic flow and hand out information on park rules and features.
■ TIP→ **If you intend to spend a lot of your holiday hiking in or simply exploring the park, consider purchasing a yearly pass for $30 (a day pass is $11).** ✉ *San Fuego 70, Arikok National Park* ☎ *297/585–1234* ⊕ *www.arubanationalpark.org* 🎫 *$11.*

★ Conchi (Natural Pool)

NATURE SIGHT | The Natural Pool, also known as "conchi," meaning "bowl," was once a very secret spot due to its remote location, but today it's well visited by many ATV, UTV, and jeep safari tours. You can also reach it by horseback or on foot from the visitor center if you're up for a two-hour hike in the hot sun. (Best to get a park ranger to guide you there.) It's not really recommended to drive there on your own, even if you have a 4x4 rental, as the roads are rough and steep, but if you do, go early in the morning to avoid the touring crowd who typically start showing up around 10 am. Regardless of the crowd, it's worth the trip—the scene of wild surf crashing over ancient black volcanic rocks into a placid aqua pool is epic, and the spray of the cold seawater shooting over the top upon you when you're swimming or snorkeling is exhilarating. A minor oil spill closed the site temporarily in September 2021. ■ TIP→ **Bring water shoes with a good grip; the rocks at the entrance to the pool are very slippery.** ✉ *Arikok National Park, Arikok National Park* ☎ *297/585–1234* ⊕ *www.aruba.com.*

Arikok National Park
and Environs

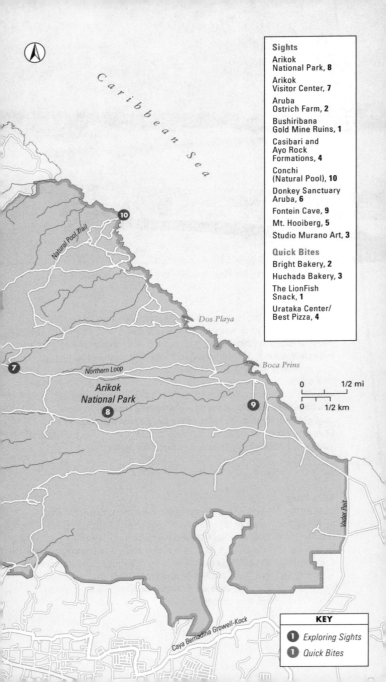

Caribbean Sea

Sights

Arikok
National Park, **8**

Arikok
Visitor Center, **7**

Aruba
Ostrich Farm, **2**

Bushiribana
Gold Mine Ruins, **1**

Casibari and
Ayo Rock
Formations, **4**

Conchi
(Natural Pool), **10**

Donkey Sanctuary
Aruba, **6**

Fontein Cave, **9**

Mt. Hooiberg, **5**

Studio Murano Art, **3**

Quick Bites

Bright Bakery, **2**

Huchada Bakery, **3**

The LionFish
Snack, **1**

Urataka Center/
Best Pizza, **4**

Natural Pool Trail

Dos Playa

Northern Loop

Boca Prins

0		1/2 mi
0		1/2 km

*Arikok
National Park*

Vader Piet

Caya Berriadma Growell-Kock

KEY	
1	*Exploring Sights*
1	*Quick Bites*

Arikok National Park's Dos Playa is a great spot for photos, picnics, and surfing.

Fontein Cave

CAVE | FAMILY | This is the park's most popular cave as it's the only one with the drawings of Arawak Indians on its ceilings. The caves are accessible during park hours, and rangers are stationed outside the cave and can provide tours that explain the history of the cave drawings as well as discuss the resident stalagmites and stalactites. The cave floor is uneven, and there can be creepy crawlies underfoot, so closed-toe shoes are encouraged. ■**TIP**➔ **If you have time, check out the two-chambered Guadirikiri Cave; sunlight pouring through holes in the cave's roof lights the space.** ✉ *Arikok National Park, off Rte 7 (Northern Loop), Arikok National Park* ☎ *297/585–1234* ⊕ *www.arubanationalpark.org.*

Beaches

Boca Prins

BEACH | You'll need a four-wheel-drive vehicle to make the trek to this strip of coastline, which is famous for its backdrop of stunning sand dunes. Near the Fontein Cave and Blue Lagoon, the beach itself is small, but with two rocky cliffs and crashing waves, it's as romantic as Aruba gets. The water is rough, and swimming is prohibited, but it's a perfect picnic stop. Wear sturdy shoes, as the entrance is rocky. **Amenities:** none. **Best for:** walking; solitude. ⊕ *Off Rte. 7A/B, near Fontein Cave.*

Exploring Arikok National Park

Visitors are free to hike on their own through Arikok National Park, and hiking maps are free at the Arikok Visitor Center. However, there's so much to see in the park in terms of flora and fauna, and so many fascinating facts about the island's fragile ecosystem and indigenous creatures, that a guide is invaluable. Luckily, free guided tours with a park ranger are available at the visitor center—reservations must be made 48 hours in advance—and are well worth it, especially for first-time visitors.

DID YOU KNOW?

Aruba is home to one of the world's rarest rattlesnakes. There are only about 200 Cascabel Rattlesnakes in existence, and they are only found naturally on this island. The park is home to the majority, but they are elusive and shy, and rarely stay out in the hot sun past 11 am. However, if you do hear a loud rattlesnake noise when you're passing a hole in the ground, don't freak out. Chances are good that it's an Aruban Burrowing Owl, or Shoco as it's known on the island. This quirky burrowing owl mimics the sound of a rattlesnake to keep predators away from its underground home.

The little red berries found on top of the Turk's Cap cactus are edible, and delicious. Just be careful if you try to pick them as these cacti are very prickly. The cacti are an important food source for the island's bird population.

Dos Playa

BEACH | One of the most photogenic picnic spots on the island, this beach is two coves divided by limestone cliffs. One is treasured by surfers for its rolling waves; the other looks placid but has a current that is far too strong for swimming—you have to settle for sunbathing only. The best access is by four-wheel drive, as it's within the boundaries of rugged Arikok National Park, but do not drive on the sand or the rocks. You might see locals surfing, but take care if you want to try as the current is very strong, and it's not for amateurs. **Amenities:** none. **Best for:** walking; solitude; surfing. ✛ *Just north of Boca Prins.*

🍴 Restaurants

Though you can get some cold drinks and small snacks at the Arikok Park Visitor Center, bring your own water as there are no food or drink outlets in the park. And please don't leave behind any litter if you bring your own food and drink.

Arikok National Park Environs: Santa Cruz and Paradera

The area surrounding Arikok National Park, including the towns of Santa Cruz and Paradera, offers offbeat attractions with unexpected animals and the island's second-highest peak, Mt. Hooiberg. There are also romantic secluded spots for picnics and unique scenic vistas for photo ops.

■ TIP→ **Make time to explore the local neighborhoods to see the cunucu (countryside) houses topped with terra-cotta-tiled roofs and often surrounded by fences made of cacti to keep the wild goats and donkeys out of the gardens.**

There are some places to grab lunch and snacks, but there aren't places to stay, shop, or go out at night, so plan to visit the area as a day trip.

Sights

Aruba Ostrich Farm

FARM/RANCH | FAMILY | Everything you ever wanted to know about the world's largest living birds can be found at this farm and ranch. There are emus, too. A large *palapa* (palm-thatched roof) houses a gift shop and restaurant that draws large bus tours, and tours of the farm are available every half hour starting at 10 am until 3 pm, seven days a week. Feeding the ostriches is fun, and you can also hold an egg in your hands. There is a full-service restaurant on-site as well as a farmer's market (check Facebook for dates), and the souvenir shop sells unique, locally made crafts and keepsakes. ⊠ *Matividiri 57, Paradera* ☎ *297/585–9630* ⊕ *www. arubaostrichfarm.com* ☜ *$14.*

Bushiribana Gold Mine Ruins

BEACH | You can view what is left of Aruba's onetime gold rush at the seaside ruins of a gold smelter; it's a great spot for photo ops. It's ironic that the Spanish left the island alone basically because they thought it was worthless; in fact, they dubbed it "isla inutil" (useless island) since they thought it had no gold or silver, but locals did find some long after the Spanish left. There is also a secret little natural pool nearby. ⊠ *North Coast, Bushiribana* ✛ *Near the California Lighthouse.*

Cunucu Houses

Pastel houses surrounded by cacti fences adorn Aruba's flat, rugged *cunucu* ("country" in Papiamento). The features of these traditional houses were developed in response to the environment. Early settlers discovered that slanting roofs allowed the heat to rise and that small windows helped to keep in the cool air. Among the earliest building materials was *caliche*, a durable calcium-carbonate substance found in the island's southeastern hills. Many houses were also built using interlocking coral rocks that didn't require mortar (this technique is no longer used, thanks to cement and concrete). Contemporary design combines some of the basic principles of the earlier homes with touches of modernization: windows, though still narrow, have been elongated; roofs are constructed of bright tiles; pretty patios have been added; and doorways and balconies present an ornamental face to the world beyond.

Casibari and Ayo Rock Formations

NATURE SIGHT | The odd-looking massive boulders at Ayo and Casibari are a mystery as they don't match the island's geological makeup in any other spot. They seem to have just cropped up out of nowhere, but they're cool to see and Casibari is fun to climb with man-made steps and handrails and tunnels set within the weird rock formation. Kids will love this all-natural jungle gym. You are not permitted to climb Ayo, but it's still worth a visit to see the ancient pictographs in a small cave (the entrance has iron bars to protect the drawings from vandalism). ⊠ *Paradera* ⊕ *www.aruba. com.*

★ Donkey Sanctuary Aruba

FARM/RANCH | **FAMILY** | Take a free tour of the island's only donkey sanctuary where volunteers help abandoned and sometimes ill wild animals enjoy a happy forever home. This is a nonprofit organization and can always use help, whether financial or with chores. You can donate there or on their website, and you can even adopt a donkey—your donation goes to its annual feed and care. Donkeys are fun, friendly animals and really enjoy visitors. It's a great family outing for all ages. ■ TIP→ **Bring carrots and apples for a really warm welcome from the residents.** ⊠ *Bringamosa, 2-Z Santa Cruz, Santa Cruz* ☎ *297/593–2933* ⊕ *main.arubandonkey.org/portal* 🎫 *Free.*

Mt. Hooiberg

MOUNTAIN | Named for its shape (hooiberg means "haystack" in Dutch), this 541-foot peak lies inland just past the airport. If you have the energy, you can climb the some 562 steps to the top for an impressive view of Oranjestad (and Venezuela on clear days). It is the island's second-highest peak; Mt. Jamanota at 617 feet is the tallest. ■TIP→ **It's a very hot climb with no shade, so wear a hat, apply plenty of sunscreen, and bring water.** ⊠ *Hooiberg 11, near Santa Cruz, Paradera.*

★ Studio Murano Art

ART GALLERY | The latest attraction in Ayo, Santa Cruz is a large, beautifully restored cunucu house that offers daily glassblowing exhibitions by a master artisan from the island of Murano, Italy, famous for its glass art. Also on the property is a large bar/restaurant with a very interesting and eclectic choice of international fare. It's an odd combination, but it really works, and it's become a popular stop for groups doing island tours. Watch free daily presentations between 11 am and 1 pm, and shop for original souvenirs on-site; you can book a workshop to make your own glass art souvenir. ⊠ *Ayo 22, Santa Cruz* ☎ *297/584–8148* ⊕ *www. facebook.com/studiomuranoartaruba* ☑ *Free.*

Coffee and Quick Bites

The interior neighborhoods of Santa Cruz, before you enter the park, and Paradera nearby, are full of little snack bars, food trucks, cafés, small restaurants, and bakeries, so seek them out for an authentic local experience while you explore another side of Aruba.

★ Bright Bakery

$ | **CAFÉ** | This landmark family-run bakery has been a local favorite since it first opened in 1949, and it's still home to the island's most authentic baked goods including epic cakes, cupcakes, and pastries. There are also sandwiches and savory snacks like *paste-chis* and hot dog *broodjes*, as well as fancy afternoon tea service, but reservations must be made 48 hours in advance for it. **Known for:** a cheery spot for breakfast; the largest collection of authentic Aruban cakes; wonderful homemade breads and buns. ⑤ *Average main: $10* ⊠ *Piedra Plat 44, Paradera* ☎ *297/585–9031* ⊕ *www. facebook.com/brightbakeryaruba.*

Huchada Bakery

$ | **BAKERY** | Located about five minutes from Arikok National Park's entrance, this is the ideal spot for authentic Aruban baked goods and snacks. There are great assorted snack boxes to-go, and a small indoor area if you feel like enjoying your treats on-site. **Known for:** local snacks like pastechis; great homemade soups; local bolos (cakes) and pastries. $ *Average main: $6* ⊠ *Santa Cruz 328, Santa Cruz.*

The Lionfish Snack

$$ | **CARIBBEAN** | "Eat 'em to beat 'em" is the motto behind this snack shack that serves only lionfish dishes to help combat the invasive species. It's only open Saturdays noon to 7:30 pm, so make sure to plan accordingly if you really want to eat here. **Known for:** lionfish wraps; lionfish fritters; lionfish wings. $ *Average main: $12* ⊠ *Paradera 100, Paradera* ⊕ *www.thelionfishsnackaruba.com* ⊗ *Closed Sun.-Fri.* ⊟ *No credit cards.*

Urataka Center / Best Pizza

$ | **BRASSERIE** | As the name suggests, this is a local favorite for pizza in Santa Cruz, but they also serve great snack platters, chicken, and burgers. There's outdoor garden seating and cold beer on tap, too. ■TIP→ **The prices** ■TIP→ **listed on the menu are in** *Aruban florin.* **Known for:** superb burgers; chicken wing baskets; specialty and create-your-own pizzas. $ *Average main: $7* ⊠ *Urataka 12 A, Santa Cruz* ⊕ *www.facebook.com/UratakaCenter.*

Chapter 8

ACTIVITIES

Updated by
Susan Campbell

On Aruba, you can hike or bike a surreal arid outback and participate in every conceivable water sport, play tennis or golf, and horseback ride along the sea. The island has also become the beach tennis capital of the Caribbean, so do give it a try while you're here. Snorkeling and diving are big of course, but there's also parasailing, banana boats, kayaking, paddleboarding, even yoga on a paddleboard, touring submarines, luxury sails, golf, and skydiving.

Aruba also has many fitness clubs that visitors are welcome to join, too. And, now there's a novel new way to enjoy Aruba's abundant nature in style with a custom luxury set up of gourmet fare and outdoor comfort provided by Picnic Aruba, the island's only licensed and official picnic company.

The island's constant trade winds also make it an ideal place to learn to windsurf and kiteboard. In fact, this island has produced world champions like 17-time world titleholder Sarah-Quita Offringa who often practices her freestyle routines at Fisherman's Huts beach.

Biking and Motorcycling

Cycling is a great way to get around the island—though biking along busy roads is not encouraged. The Linear Park paved trail from downtown Oranjestad to the airport or from Fisherman's Huts beach to Malmok is ideal for families seeking a biking adventure along the sea. Green Bike kiosks dot the island making it easy to grab a bike and deposit it at another station when you're done. If you'd rather cycle with less exertion, there are electric-bike rentals, too. Many resorts offer their guests coaster bikes for free (or for a low fee) to pedal around the beach areas, and there are also guided mountain bike tours that take you to the rugged interior. Or let your hair down completely and cruise around on a Harley-Davidson, either solo or with a group tour.

Relatively flat, Aruba can be the perfect biking destination.

Rentals

There are plenty of dealers who will be happy to help you in your motoring pursuits.

George's Cycle Co

BIKING | This outfit has been renting motorcycles, scooters, and ATVs since the late 1980s. It's a reputable firm that offers great vehicles at good prices. Hotel pickup and drop-off is available. ⊠ *L. G. Smith Blvd. 124,* ☎ *297/593–2202* ⊕ *www.georgecycles.com* ✉ *From $55 per day.*

★ Green Bike Aruba

BIKING | It's no surprise that the first bike-sharing program in the Caribbean became popular very quickly, since Aruba is a Dutch-influenced island and people from the Netherlands adore their bikes. With more than 100 modern bikes at eight stations dotting the island (at busy tourist junctions including the cruise terminal), it's easy to swipe your credit card and hit the road. When you're done, park it somewhere else for the next person. Rentals are by the hour, but three-, five-, and seven-day passes and annual memberships are also available, as are guided bike tours. ⊠ *Caya Ernesto Petronia Ponton 69, Oranjestad* ☎ *297/594–6368* ⊕ *www. greenbikearuba.com* ✉ *From $15 (2 hours).*

Organized Excursions

Aruba Active Vacations Mountain Biking Tours

BIKING | FAMILY | Unless you are a skilled cyclist, it's best to join a tour to explore the island's arid, rugged, and unforgiving outback. This outfitter offers 2-hour guided tours and private tours on top-quality Cannondale bikes with water and helmets supplied, including pickup and drop-off at your hotel. Points of interest include Alto Vista Chapel and the California Lighthouse, and the tour begins at the company's windsurfing shop at Fisherman's Huts. You can also rent the Cannondale bikes on your own. ⊠ *Fisherman's Huts Beach, Malmokweg* ☎ *297/586–0989* ⊕ *www. aruba-active-vacations.com* 🎫 *From $60 (minimum 2 people).*

Bird-Watching

★ Birdwatching Aruba

BIRD WATCHING | The intimate outfit is run by Michiel Oversteegen, an award-winning professional wildlife photographer who can arrange private birding or nature photo tours with photo instruction as well. Tours are good for beginning birders as well as the most avid ornithologist, or anyone who wants to discover the island's surprisingly eclectic and abundant selection of birds. ■**TIP→ Pickup and drop-off included, but a max of five people allowed with a minimum of four hours; online booking only.** ⊠ *Oranjestad* ☎ *297/699–2075* ⊕ *www.birdwatchingaruba.com.*

Bowling

★ Dream Bowl Aruba

BOWLING | FAMILY | Dream Bowl does it right with eight glow-in-the-dark bowling lanes, hip music, computerized scoring, a video arcade, a food court, and prize machines. It opens after 4 pm. ⊠ *Palm Beach Plaza, L. G. Smith Blvd. 95, Suite 310, Palm Beach* ☎ *297/280–8888* ⊕ *www.facebook.com/Dreambowl* 🎫 *From $22* ☉ *Closed Thurs.*

Eagle Bowling Palace

BOWLING | FAMILY | Arubans love to bowl and often compete off-island. The Eagle emporium is the local favorite spot. Close to the high-rise strip, it has computerized lanes, a snack bar, a cocktail lounge, and occasional big screen bingo. Equipment rentals and group rates are available. It opens after 3 pm. ⊠ *Sasakiweg, Pos*

Abao ☎ *297/583–5038* ⊕ *www.facebook.com/eagle.bowling.9*
🎫 *From $20 per lane per hour* 🕙 *Closed Mon.*

Day Sails

Aruba is not much of a sailing destination—the marina is tiny by many Caribbean island standards—but they are big on luxury catamarans taking large groups out for a fun day of party sailing, snorkeling tours, or sunset dinner cruises. The weather is typically ideal, the waters are calm and clear, and the trade winds are gentle, so there's never really a bad time to hit the waves.

The main operators are DePalm, Red Sail, and Pelican. All have large catamarans, but some companies also offer old-fashioned wooden schooners for their day sails and snorkeling trips like Jolly Pirates and Sail Away. A few smaller private yacht charters are available as well. Many tours include stops for snorkeling and often include drinks, snacks, loud music, and sometimes sunset dinners.

Day sails usually take off from either DePalm Pier, Hadicurari Pier, or Pelican Pier on Palm Beach. Many tour companies include pickup and drop-off services at major resorts that are not on Palm Beach.

★ Jolly Pirates
SNORKELING | FAMILY | Aruba's unique, pirate-themed sailing adventure is a rollicking ride aboard a big, beautiful teak schooner complete with a wild and crazy swashbuckling crew and an open bar. The ships offer snorkeling tours with two or three stops and a rope-swing adventure, and the sunset cruises are also first-rate. Prepare to party hearty (it's basically impossible not to) due to their signature "pirate's poison" rum punch and infectious loud music. Snorkel trips always include the *Antilla* wreck. Departures are from Hadicurari Pier beside MooMba Beach Bar. ⊠ *Hadicurari Pier, Palm Beach* ✛ *Office behind MooMba Beach Bar* ☎ *586–8107* ⊕ *www.jolly-pirates.com* 🎫 *From $33 (sunset sail) $52 (snorkel sail).*

Montforte III
SAILING | Take your sailing experience up a notch aboard this luxurious teak schooner that is designed to pamper. Exclusive tours take you to spots like Spanish Lagoon for snorkeling and kayaking, and around Boca Catalina for four-course dinners under the stars. Unlimited premium spirits, signature cocktails, tapas, and snacks

Snorkeling from a replica pirate ship will thrill any swashbuckler.

are included in all trips, and there's sometimes live music onboard as well. Departure is from Pelican Pier. ✉ *Pelican Pier, Palm Beach* ☎ *297/583–0400* ⊕ *www.monfortecruise.com* ✉ *From $139.*

★ Octopus Aruba

SAILING | Octopus has been offering group and private snorkel and party sails on their catamaran for decades, but now they also offer a whole new experience with a fleet of cool "aqua donut" boats. The donuts seat up to 10 people on a comfy padded bench circling a large table; you can captain it yourself or have it crewed. Stable and easy to navigate, the aqua donut won't sink even if it's full of water. Octopus offers two very unique catered adventures aboard them—a luxury brunch and snorkel outing, and a gourmet dinner sunset cruise. It's like having your own table and floating bar on the sea, but they call it your own "private island."✉ *Palm Beach* ⊹ *Orange beach hut between the Playa Linda and Holiday Inn* ☎ *297/560–6565* ⊕ *octopusaruba.com* ✉ *From $69.99.*

Sailaway Tours Aruba

SAILING | At 110 feet, the *Lady Black* is a beautifully retrofitted old-fashioned wooden schooner that's also the island's largest party ship. Enjoy an open bar and a big rope hammock on the bow while you sail with one of their snorkel, sunset, or dinner cruises. The friendly crew is happy to help you try some antics on the rope swing, and you can even hop on their backs while they do flips into the water. The party can get crazy. Available for private

charters as well. ⊠ *Hadicurari Pier, Palm Beach* ⊹ *Look for their sign to check in across from MooMba Beach Bar in front of Hadicurari Pier* ☎ *297/739–9000* ⊕ *www.sailawaytour.com* ✆ *From $60.*

★ Tranquilo Charters Aruba

SAILING | Captain Mike Hagedoorn, a legendary Aruban sailor, handed the helm over to his son Captain Anthony a few years ago after 20 years of running the family business. Today, *The Tranquilo*—a 43-foot sailing yacht—still takes small groups of passengers to a secluded spot at a Spanish lagoon named Mike's Reef, where not many other snorkel trips venture. The lunch cruise to the south side always includes "Mom's famous Dutch pea soup," and they also do private charters for dinner sails and sailing trips around Aruba's lesser-explored coasts. Look for the red boat docked at the Renaissance Marina beside the Atlantis Submarine launch. ⊠ *Renaissance Marina, Oranjestad* ☎ *297/586-1418* ⊕ *www.tranquiloaruba.com* ✆ *From $100.*

Fishing

Deep-sea catches here include anything from barracuda, tuna, and wahoo to kingfish, sailfish, and marlins. A few skippered charter boats are available for half- or full-day excursions. Package prices vary but typically include tackle, bait, and refreshments.

★ Driftwood Charters

FISHING | Driftwood is a tournament-rigged, 35-foot yacht manned by Captain Herby, who is famous for offering deep-sea fishing charters on Aruba since the early 1990s. He is also co-owner of Driftwood Restaurant and is always happy to bring your catch to their chef for expert preparation so you can enjoy it for dinner the very same night. Charters can accommodate up to six people. ⊠ *Seaport Marina, Oranjestad* ☎ *297/583–2515* ⊕ *www.driftwoodfishingcharters.com/* ✆ *From $400.*

Teaser Fishing Charters Aruba

FISHING | FAMILY | The expertise of the Teaser crew is matched by a commitment to sensible fishing practices, which include catch and release and avoiding ecologically sensitive areas. The company's yacht is fully equipped, and the crew seem to have an uncanny ability to locate the best fishing spots with Captain Milton at the helm. ⊠ *Renaissance Marina, Oranjestad* ☎ *297/593–9228* ⊕ *www.teaserfishingaruba.com* ✆ *From $400 (limit 6 people).*

Golf

Golf may seem incongruous on an arid island such as Aruba, yet there are two popular courses.

The Links at Divi Aruba

GOLF | This 9-hole course was designed by Karl Litten and Lorie Viola. The par-36 flat layout stretches to 2,952 yards and features paspalum grass (best for seaside courses) and takes you past beautiful lagoons. It's a testy little course with water abounding, making accuracy more important than distance. Amenities include a golf school with professional instruction, a driving range, a practice green, and a two-story golf clubhouse with a pro shop. ⊠ *Divi Village Golf & Beach Resort, J. E. Irausquin Blvd. 93, Druif* ☎ *297/581–4653* ⊕ *www.divilinks.com* ⊠ *From $96, after 3pm $79* 🏌 *9 holes, 2952 yards, par 36.*

★ Tierra del Sol

GOLF | Stretching out to 6,811 yards, this stunning course is situated on the northwest coast near the California Lighthouse and is Aruba's only 18-hole course. Designed by Robert Trent Jones Jr., Tierra del Sol combines Aruba's native beauty (cacti and rock formations, stunning views) with good greens and beautiful landscaping. Wind can also be a factor here on the rolling terrain, as are the abundant bunkers and water hazards. Greens fees include a golf cart equipped with GPS and a communications system that allows you to order drinks for your return to the clubhouse. The fully stocked golf shop is one of the Caribbean's most elegant, with an extremely attentive staff. This course hosts numerous events including the annual Aruba International Pro-Am Golf Tournament every August. ⊠ *Tierra del Sol Resort, Caya di Solo 10, Malmok-weg* ☎ *297/586–7800* ⊕ *www.tierradelsol.com/golf* ⊠ *From $89 for 9 holes high season* 🏌 *18 holes, 6811 yards, par 71.*

Hiking

Despite Aruba's arid landscape, hiking the rugged countryside will give you the best opportunities to see the island's wildlife and flora. Arikok National Park is an excellent place to glimpse the real Aruba, free of the trappings of tourism. The heat can be oppressive, so be sure to take it easy, wear a hat, and have a bottle of water handy. Get maps and information at Arikok National Park Visitor Center.

■ TIP→ **Guided hikes are recommended for those with little hiking experience.**

Beyond Arikok National Park, the 500-step trek up Mt. Hooiberg (locals call it "The Haystack") is also a good workout that rewards with fabulous island views.

★ Arikok National Park

HIKING & WALKING | FAMILY | There are more than 20 miles of trails concentrated in the island's eastern interior and along its northeastern coast. Arikok Park is crowned by Aruba's second-highest mountain, the 577-foot Mt. Arikok, so you can also go climbing there. Hiking in the park, whether alone or in a group led by guides, is generally not too strenuous, but it is hot. You'll need sturdy shoes to grip the granular surfaces and climb the occasionally steep terrain. You should also exercise caution with the strong sun—bring along plenty of water and wear sunscreen and a hat. At the park's main entrance, the Arikok Visitor Center houses exhibits, restrooms, and snack concessions, and provides maps and marked trail information, park rules, and features. Free guided minitours are the best way to get oriented at the park entrance. Tour operators also offer four-wheeling and horseback tours across the rugged Arikok landscape. You can also download hiking maps from their website for self-guided tours. ✉ *Santa Cruz* ☎ *297/585–1234* ⊕ *www.arubanationalpark.org* 🖃 *$11 park entrance, $28 year pass* ☼ *Park closes at 4 pm.*

Horseback Riding

Ranches offer short jaunts along the beach or longer rides through the countryside and even to the ruins of an old gold mill. Riders of all experience levels will be thrilled that most of Aruba's horses are descendants of the Spanish Paso Fino—meaning "fine step"— which offer a supersmooth ride even at a trot!

★ Rancho Loco

HORSEBACK RIDING | FAMILY | Surrounded by a lush fruit and vegetable farm, Rancho Loco is touted as the "greenest ranch in Aruba." This equestrian center also gives lessons and boards and trains horses. Their tours range from sunset jaunts on Moro Beach to Arikok Park interior treks including trips to the Natural Pool. Private rides also available. ✉ *Sombre 22-e, Santa Cruz* ☎ *297/592–6039* ⊕ *www.rancholocoaruba.com/en* ☞ *From $95.*

Jet Skiing

There are about half a dozen spots to book Jet Skis or wave run-ners along Palm Beach including the *family-run, full-service water sports outfitter, Aruba Watersports Centre (see Recommended Dive Operators under Scuba Diving and Snorkeling).*

Kayaking

Kayaking is a popular sport on Aruba, especially because the waters are so calm. It's a great way to explore the coast and the mangroves.

Aruba Outdoor Adventures

KAYAKING | FAMILY | This small, family-run outfitter offers a unique combination of small-group (six people max) pedal-kayaking and snorkel tours along the island's southeastern coast. Mangroves and reef explorations take you around calm water near Mangel Halto, Savaneta, and Barcadera; well-informed guides explain the natural environment and help guests navigate the snorkeling portions. No kayaking experience is necessary. Pickup and drop-off are included, as well as snorkel equipment, a dry bag, snacks, and drinks. Departures are from the DePalm Island Ferry Terminal outside Oranjestad. ⊠ *DePalm Island Ferry Terminal, Balashi* ☎ *297/749–6646* ⊕ *www.arubaoutdooradventures.com* ⊠ *From $80.*

★ Clear Kayak Aruba

KAYAKING | FAMILY | This is the only Aruba outfitter that offers clear-bottom sea kayaks, and the only one offering night tours as well. By day, groups paddle through the natural mangroves at Mangel Halto with a guide who can tell you how the roots create a natural nursery for juvenile marine life; the route also passes over lots of big, healthy coral full of colorful tropical fish. A second tour begins at Arashi Beach at dusk; then, after dark, the kayaks are lit up with LED lights that attract marine life to their clear bottoms. You must be age 12 or older to participate. ⊠ *Savaneta 402, Savaneta* ☎ *297/566–2205* ⊕ *www.clearkayakaruba.com* ⊠ *From $65.*

The calm waters and mangrove lagoons found along Aruba's southern coast are perfect for kayaking.

Multisport Outfitters

There are a number of outfitters in Aruba that can handle nearly all of your water or land-based activities with guided excursions and rental equipment. Here is a list of a few of our favorites.

Around Aruba Tours

SPECIAL-INTEREST TOURS | Spearheaded by Philip Merryweather, owner of Philip's Animal Garden, this tour operator likes to do things a little differently, focusing on education and ecoconservation as much as possible while still offering adrenaline rush explorations in a variety of vehicles; they promise to bring you to the island's best hidden natural gems and vistas. They also offer private luxury boat tours. ⊠ *Alto Vista 116, Noord* ☎ *297/593–6363* ⊕ *www.aroundarubatours.com* ✉ *From $60.*

Aruba Nature Explorers

ECOTOURISM | The newest way to explore the island's nature and enchanting secret spots are on this outfitter's unique themed tours like the sunrise hike and beach meditation at Alto Vista or the mangrove hiking trail through Spanish Lagoon. There's also a tour that teaches guests about Aruba's surprising gold rush history with an enlightening guided hike through Bushiribana. Breakfast or lunch is often included in the price. ⊠ *Italiestraat 50, Oranjestad* ☎ *297/731–0077* ⊕ *arubaeco.tours* ✉ *From $105.*

★ De Palm Tours

BOATING | FAMILY | Aruba's premier tour company covers every inch of the island on land and under sea, and they even have their own submarine (Atlantis) and semi-submarine (*Seaworld Explorer*) and their own all-inclusive private island destination (De Palm Island), which has great snorkeling as well as Seatrek, a cool underwater air-supplied-helmet walk. Land exploration options include air-conditioned bus sightseeing tours and rough and rugged outback jaunts by jeep safari to popular attractions like the natural pool. You can also do off-road tours in a UTV (two-seater utility task vehicle) via their guided caravan trips. On the waves, their luxury catamaran *De Palm Pleasure* offers romantic sunset sails and snorkel trips that include an option to try SNUBA—deeper snorkeling with an air-supplied raft at Aruba's most famous shipwreck. De Palm also offers airport transfers and private VIP transfers. ✉ *L. G. Smith Blvd. 142, Oranjestad* ☎ *297/582—4400* ⊕ *www.depalmtours.com/.*

EL Tours

This tour and transfer company offers a wide range of tours to explore Aruba including hiking, UTV tours, beach-hopping jaunts, jeep safaris, and island highlights. Personalized custom tours and VIP airport transfers are also available. ✉ *Barcadera 4, Oranjestad* ☎ *297/585–6730* ⊕ *www.eltoursaruba.com.*

Pelican Adventures

SAILING | FAMILY | This family-owned tour and water sports company has been in operation since 1984 and today they are one of the island's largest activity hubs; they've also partnered with some of the island's smaller operators to offer every conceivable way to explore this island on land and sea. They also have their own pier and dining spot on Palm Beach. They really are a one-stop-shop for adventure on Aruba. ✉ *Pelican Pier, Palm Beach* ⊹ *Near the Holiday Inn and Playa Linda hotels* ☎ *297/586–3271* ⊕ *www.pelican-aruba.com* ⛴ *From $59.*

★ Red Sail Sports Aruba

BOATING | A dynamic company established in 1989, they are experts in the field of water-sports recreation. They offer excellent diving excursions and instruction, snorkel sails, sunset sails, and full dinner sails, and they are the premier spot for Jetlev (jetpacks over the water), jet blades, and hoverboards with instruction (weekdays). The company also has its own sports equipment shops and you can now book many land excursions through them. ✉ *J. E. Irausquin Blvd. 348-A, Palm Beach* ☎ *297/523–1600* ⊕ *www.redsailaruba.com.*

Aruba is known as one of the Caribbean's wreck diving capitals.

Parasailing

For about 12 exhilarating minutes, motorboats at Palm and Eagle beaches tow you up and over the waters around Aruba—single or tandem rides are available. You can make arrangements with your hotel or through independent operators like Aruba Watersports Centre on Palm Beach (*see Recommended Dive Operators under Scuba Diving and Snorkeling*).

Scuba Diving and Snorkeling

With visibility of up to 90 feet, the waters around Aruba are excellent for snorkeling and diving. In fact, Aruba is known as one of the wreck diving capitals of the Caribbean. Advanced and novice divers alike will find plenty to occupy their time, as many of the most popular sites—including some interesting shipwrecks—are found in shallow waters ranging from 30 to 60 feet. Coral reefs covered with sensuously waving sea fans and eerie giant sponge tubes attract a colorful menagerie of sea life, including gliding manta rays, curious sea turtles, shy octopuses, and fish from grunts to groupers. Marine preservation is a priority on Aruba, and regulations by the Conference on International Trade in Endangered Species make it unlawful to remove coral, conch, and other marine life from the water.

Day sail operators often offer snorkeling, and it's usually coupled with an open bar and loud music; almost all of them stop at the famous *Antilla* shipwreck just offshore, which provides a rare treat for snorkelers to be able to view a wreck typically only divers would be able to access. Some dive operators also allow snorkelers to tag along with divers on a trip for a lower fee as well.

Major West-Side Dive Sites

Airplane Wrecks. Two planes purposely scuttled to create a new dive site are still somewhat intact around Renaissance Private Island. You must do a drift dive to see them; they broke apart somewhat after Hurricane Lenny caused big swells in the area.

***Antilla* Wreck.** This German freighter, which sank off the northwest coast near Malmok Beach, is popular with both divers and snorkelers. Some outfits also offer SNUBA, which allows you to get a bit closer to the wreck if you are not certified to dive. When Germany declared war on the Netherlands in 1940 during World War II it was stationed off the coast where it still is now. The captain chose to sink the ship on purpose before Aruban officials could board and seize it. The 400-foot-long vessel—referred to by locals as "the ghost ship"— broke into two distinct halves. It has large compartments, and you can climb into the captain's bathtub, which sits beside the wreck, for a unique photo op. Lobster, angelfish, yellowtail, and other fish swim about the wreck, which is blanketed by giant tube sponges and coral.

Black Beach. The clear waters just off this beach are dotted with sea fans. The area takes its name from the rounded black stones lining the shore. It's the only bay on the island's north coast sheltered from thunderous waves, making it a safe spot for diving.

***Californian* Wreck.** Although this steamer is submerged at a depth that's perfect for underwater photography, this site is safe only for advanced divers; the currents here are strong, and the waters are dangerously choppy. This wreck is what the famous lighthouse is named for.

Malmok Reef (*Debbie II* Wreck). Lobsters and stingrays are among the highlights at this bottom reef adorned by giant green, orange, and purple barrel sponges as well as leaf and brain coral. From here you can spot the *Debbie II,* a 120-foot barge that sank in 1992.

***Pedernales* Wreck.** During World War II, this oil tanker was torpe-doed by a German submarine. The U.S. military cut out the dam-aged centerpiece, towed the two remaining pieces to the States, and welded them together into a smaller vessel that eventually transported troops during the invasion of Normandy. The section that was left behind in shallow water is now surrounded by coral formations, making this a good site for novice divers. The ship's cabins, washbasins, and pipelines are exposed. The area teems with grouper and angelfish. It's also a good site for snorkelers since it's easily visible from the shallows.

Tugboat Wreck. Spotted eagle rays and stingrays are sometimes observed at this shipwreck at the foot of Harbour Reef, which is one of Aruba's most popular. Spectacular formations of brain, sheet, and star coral blanket the path to the wreck, which is inhabited by several bright-green moray eels.

East-Side Dive Sites

***Jane C.* Wreck.** This 200-foot freighter, lodged in an almost vertical position at a depth of 90 feet, is near the coral reef west of De Palm Island. Night diving is exciting here, as the polyps emerge from the corals that grow profusely on the steel plates of the decks and cabins. Soft corals and sea fans are also abundant in the area. The current is strong, and this is for advanced divers only.

Punta Basora. This narrow reef stretches far into the sea off the island's easternmost point. On calm days you'll see eagle rays, stingrays, barracudas, and hammerhead sharks, as well as hawks-bill and loggerhead turtles.

The Wall. From May to August, green sea turtles intent on laying their eggs abound at this steep-walled reef. You'll also spot groupers and burrfish swimming nearby. Close to shore, massive sheet corals are plentiful; in the upper part of the reef are colorful varieties such as black coral, star coral, and flower coral. Flitting about are brilliant damselfish, rock beauties, and porgies.

Recommended Dive Operators

★ Aruba Watersports Center
DIVING & SNORKELING | FAMILY | This family-run, full-service water sports outfitter is right on Palm Beach, offering a comprehen-sive variety of adventures including small group PADI dives and snorkeling trips, but also WaveRunners, tubing, Hobie Cat sailing,

stand-up paddleboarding, kayaking, wakeboarding, and parasailing. Snorkeling trips aboard the *Arusun* are for small groups, and the boat goes to spots others don't, including the *Pedernales* wreck. ⊠ *L. G. Smith Blvd. 81B, Palm Beach* ⊹ *Between Barcelo and Hilton resorts* ☎ *297/586–6613* ⊕ *www.arubawatersportscenter.com* 🖃 *From $20.*

★ JADS Dive Center

SCUBA DIVING | Owned by the local Fang family, JADS has been in operation for decades and is famous for its intro to dive package that takes you to one of the island's only shore diving sites at Mangel Halto, which has easy access for beginners. JADS also offers all levels of PADI dive instruction, a children's program, personalized boat dive trips, and guided night dives. Located right on Baby Beach, there's a full-service dive shop with snorkel equipment rentals. Rum Reef, an adult-only infinity pool bar also owned by the family is right next door. ■ TIP→ **Looking for a unique souvenir? One dive instructor sells handmade jewelry made from lionfish skin in the dive shop; the craft helps rid the environment of these destructive fish.** ⊠ *Seroe Colorado 245E, Seroe Colorado* ☎ *297/584–6070* ⊕ *www.jadsaruba.com* 🖃 *From $58.*

Native Divers Aruba

SCUBA DIVING | A small, personal operation, Native Divers Aruba specializes in PADI open-water courses. Ten different certification options include specialties like Multilevel Diver, Search & Recovery Diver, and Underwater Naturalist. Their boat schedule is also flexible, and it's easy to tailor instruction to your specific needs. They also allow snorkelers to tag along and provide all the necessary equipment. ⊠ *Marriott Surf Club, Palm Beach* ⊹ *On the beach in front of Marriott Surf Club* ☎ *297/586–4763* ⊕ *www.nativedivers.com* 🖃 *From $80.*

S.E. Aruba Fly 'n Dive

SCUBA DIVING | One of the island's oldest diving operators, S.E. Aruba Fly 'n Dive offers a full range of PADI courses as well as many specialty courses like Nitrox Diver, Wreck Diver, and Deep Diver. Private snorkeling trips are available, and they can also instruct you in rescue techniques, becoming an underwater naturalist, or underwater photography. ⊠ *L. G. Smith Blvd. 1A, Oranjestad* ☎ *297/588–1150* ⊕ *www.se-aruba.com* 🖃 *From $100.*

Skydiving

★ SkyDive Aruba

SKYDIVING | There's nothing like the adrenaline rush when you are forced to jump out of a perfectly good airplane at 10,000 feet because you are attached to your instructor. You have no choice but to free-fall at 120 mph toward the island for 35 seconds until your chute opens, and then your downward journey has you floating to the sand in a little over five minutes. Afterward you can purchase a video of your courageous leap. Group discounts are available. Hotel pickup and drop-off are included. ☒ *Malmok Beach, Malmokweg* ☎ *297/735–0654* ⊕ *www.skydivearuba. com* 🖃 *From $299* ☞ *The minimum age is 13 and the minimum weight is 100 lbs.*

Submarine Excursions

★ Atlantis Submarines

ENTERTAINMENT CRUISE | **FAMILY** | Enjoy the deep without getting wet in a real U.S. Coast Guard–approved submarine with *Atlantis,* run by De Palm Tours and operating on the island for over 25 years. The underwater reefs are teeming with marine life, and the 65-foot air-conditioned sub takes up to 48 passengers for a voyage 130 feet into the deep to view shipwrecks and amazing sights with informative narration. The company also owns the *Seaworld Explorer,* a semisubmersible that allows you to sit and view Aruba's marine habitat from 5 feet below the surface. (Children must be a minimum of 36 inches tall and four years old.) ☒ *Renaissance Marina, L. G. Smith Blvd. 82, Oranjestad* ☎ *297/522–4400* ⊕ *www.depalmtours.com/submarine-tours* 🖃 *Sub from $105, Seaworld Explorer from $45.*

Water Parks

Aruba doesn't have a lot of public parks or playgrounds with swings and jungle-gym type of equipment around the tourism areas, but there are some great water-park options for a day off the resort that adults will enjoy as much as children.

★ De Palm Island Water Park

WATER SPORTS | **FAMILY** | Part of the all-inclusive program of a De Palm private island is the big colorful signature water park, which is great for all ages, including toddlers. An adults-only water park

Did You Know?

Aruba native Sarah-Quita Najive Offringa started windsurfing at age 9 at Fisherman's Hut Beach. Today, at age 28, she has won 16 world championship titles.

opened in late 2019, and ziplining over the park is also an option. Food and drink, snorkeling equipment, and banana boat rides are included. They also have their own resident flock of flamingoes on-site. Pickup and drop-off are available. ⊠ *De Palm Island Ferry Terminal, De Palm Island Way Z/N, Oranjestad* ⊹ *Free water taxi from pier to the island* ☎ *297/522–4400* ⊕ *www.depalmisland. com* ⬛ *From $89 including bus; from $85 no bus.*

Windsurfing and Kiteboarding

Aruba has ideal conditions for windsurfing: trade winds that average 20 knots year-round and calm azure-blue waters. With a few lessons from a certified instructor, even novices will be jibing in no time. The southwestern coast's tranquil waters at Fisherman's Huts make it ideal for both beginners and intermediates, as the winds are steady and sudden gusts are rare. Experts will find Grapefield and Boca Grandi beaches more challenging; winds are fierce and often shift without warning.

Kiteboarding has also become all the rage on Aruba. The sport involves gliding on and above the water on a small surfboard or wakeboard while hooked up to an inflatable kite. Windsurfing experience helps, and practice time on the beach is essential, but these are different sports. You can watch the colorful kites flying all around Fisherman's Huts Beach, where boarders practice and give lessons. Pros will tell you to carve out at least four hours for your first lesson on the beach. And the new sport of "wing foiling" has now officially taken flight on the island, too. It's a surfboard with a fin (foil) attached to the bottom of it and a handheld sail gives you the power to slice through the waves. Bizarre, but fun.

Each year, usually in July, the Hi-Winds Pro-Am Windsurfing Competition attracts professionals and amateurs from around the world. There are divisions for women, men, juniors, masters, and grand masters. Disciplines include slalom, course racing, long distance, and freestyle. The event has become one big week-long beach party with entertainment and additional events that go day and night. No doubt there will be hydrofoil competitions there soon, too.

★ Aruba Active Vacations

WATER SPORTS | FAMILY | Located on Fisherman's Huts beach—the best spot on the island for optimum wind and wave conditions—this operation has been the go-to for many years as THE best place to learn windsurfing, and, more recently, kiteboarding. Local alums of their school include world-class competitors like

Women's Windsurf Champion Sarah-Quita Offringa, and their expert instructors ensure even first-timers are riding the waves in no time. They also offer mountain biking and stand-up paddleboarding, and they are the only outfit on the island that does "blokarting"—sail-powered land carting. ⊠ *L. G. Smith Blvd. 486, Palm Beach* ✛ *On Fisherman's Huts Beach* ☎ *297/586–0989* ⊕ *www.aruba-active-vacations.com* 🎫 *From $60.*

★ Vela Aruba

WINDSURFING | **FAMILY** | All kinds of sporty fun-in-the-sun options are available at this fun and funky kiosk in the sand, including professional windsurfing and kiteboarding lessons, and they are the first official operator to offer "wing foiling" lessons. You can rent sea kayaks and stand-up paddleboards (and take lessons in both; instructors even offer yoga on stand-up paddleboards) and they also have zayaking, which combines the best of snorkeling and kayaking in one cool floating contraption that lets you see underwater through a screen while you float. But if you'd rather plant your feet in the sand to do your yoga, they offer that too as well as beach boot camps. ⊠ *L. G. Smith Blvd. 101, Palm Beach* ✛ *Between the Aruba Marriott and the Ritz-Carlton* ☎ *297/586–3735* ⊕ *www.velaaruba.com* 🎫 *Rentals from $35, lessons from $60.*

Index

Photo Credits

Front Cover: Michael DeFreitas Caribbean/Alamy [Description: Snorkelling tour off Malmok Beach, Aruba.]. **Back cover, from left to right:** littlenySTOCK/Shutterstock, littlenySTOCK/Shutterstock, Chiyacat/Shutterstock. Spine: Damsea/Shutterstock. **Interior, from left to right:** MasterPhoto/Shutterstock (1). David Troeger/Aruba Tourism Authority (2). **Chapter 1: Experience Aruba:** Aruba Tourism Authority (6-7). littlenySTOCK/Shutterstock (8-9). Corey Weiner/Red Square, Inc. (9). Göran Ingman [CC BY-SA 2.0]/Flickr (9). Jack Jackson/Agefotostock (10). Aruba Tourism Authority (10). ARTN Photography (10). Aruba Tourism Authority (10). Aruba Tourism Authority (11). Aruba Tourism Authority (11). Rebecca Genin/Aruba Tourism (12). Aruba Tourism Authority (12). Passions on the Beach (12). Courtesy of Kukoo Kunuku (12). Aruba Tourism Authority (13). Vilainecrevette/Shutterstock (13). Aruba Tourism Authority (16). Jetlag Creative Studio (16). ARTN Photography (16). Aruba Tourism Authority (16). Aruba Tourism Authority (17). Kenny Theysen/Aruba Ocean Villas (18). Don Riddle Images (18). Bucuti & Tara Beach Resort (18). Divi Aruba Phoenix Beach Resort (18). Hilton (19). Aruba Tourism Authority (20). Cado de Lannoy/Aruba Active Vacations (20). TIERRA DEL SOL (20). Aruba Tourism Authority (20). Aruba Tourism Authority (21). Hans Wagemaker/Shutterstock (30). **Chapter 3: Oranjestad:** dbvirago/iStockphoto (63). Birdiegal/Shutterstock (68). Donaldford/Dreamstime (70-71). Kenneth Theysen/Timeless-Pixx (75). littlenySTOCK/Shutterstock (85). Ian Mackenzie [CC BY 2.0]/Flickr (89). **Chapter 4: Manchebo, Druif, and Eagle Beaches:** Kjersti Joergensen/Dreamstime (91). fmbackx/iStockphoto (96-97). Amsterdam Manor Beach Resort Aruba (105). Bucuti Beach Resort (106). **Chapter 5: Palm Beach and Noord and Western Tip (California Dunes):** DiegoMariottini/Shutterstock (111). Madame Janette's (122). Corey Weiner/Red Square, Inc. (128). scott lowden/Aruba Tourism Authority (137). sbossert/iStockphoto (140). littlenySTOCK/Shutterstock (142-143). **Chapter 6: San Nicolas and Savaneta:** Aruba Tourism Authority (145). Aruba Tourism Authority (150). Kjersti Joergensen/Shutterstock (153). Steve Photography/Shutterstock (159). **Chapter 7: Arikok National Park and Environs:** Aruba Tourism Authority (161). Aruba Tourism Authority (165). Aruba Tourism Authority (168). Paul D'Innocenzo (172-173). **Chapter 8: Activities:** Steve Photography/Shutterstock (177). Corey Weiner/Red Square, Inc. (179). Corey Weiner/Red Square, Inc. (182). Marriott (187). Rebecca Genin/Aruba Tourism (189). Armando Goedgedrag (194-195). Paul D'Innocenzo (197). **About Our Writer:** photo courtesy of the author.

*Every effort has been made to trace the copyright holders, and we apologize in advance for any accidental errors. We would be happy to apply the corrections in the following edition of this publication.

Notes

Notes